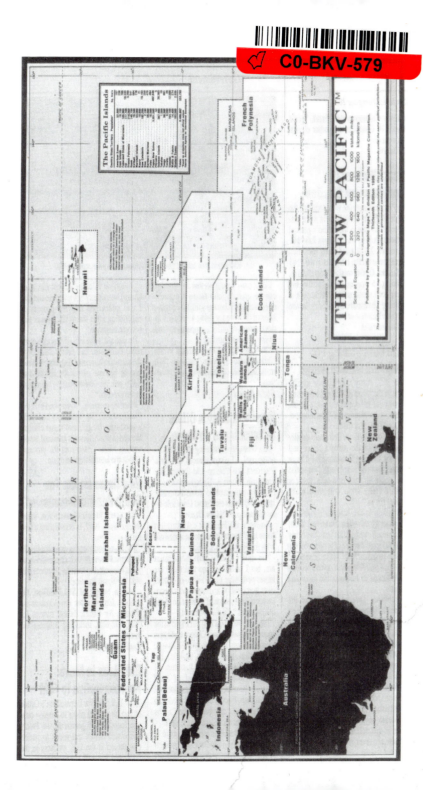

THE NEW PACIFIC™

Scale at Equator

Published by Pacific Geographic Maps™, a division of Pacific Magazine Corporation.
Thirteenth Edition 1998

AMERICAN SAMOA

TUTUILA ISLAND

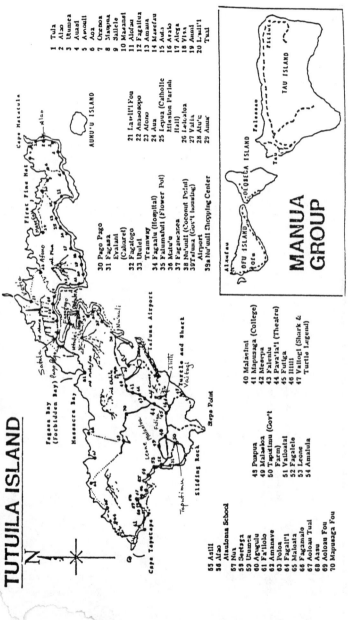

1 Tula
2 Alao
3 Utumea
4 Auasi
5 Aoaull
6 Aoa
7 Onenoa
8 Sialega
9 Sailele
10 Masanei
11 Alofau
12 Fagaitua
13 Amaua
14 Masefau
15 Auto
16 Afono
17 Alega
18 Vatia
19 Amani
20 Leull'i Tuai

21 Leull'i Fou
22 Anaoaapo
23 Afono
24 Aua
25 Leppa (Catholic Mission Parish Hall)
26 Leteloa
27 Vatia
28 Atu'u
29 Aua'

30 Pago Pago
31 Fagasa (Cabaret)
  Eyalani
32 Fagatogo
33 Utulei
  Tramway
34 Fagaalu (Hospital)
35 Fatumafuti (Flower Pot)
36 Matu'u
37 Faganeanea
38 Nu'uuli (Coconut Point) Airport
39 Tafuna (Gov't housing)
39a Nu'uuli Shopping Center

40 Malaeimi
41 Mapusaga (College)
42 Mesepa
43 Faleniu
44 Pava'la'l (Theatre)
45 Futiga
46 Illili
47 Vaitogi (Shark & Turtle Legend)

48 Puapua
49 Malaeloa
50 Tapatimu (Gov't Farm)
51 Vailoatai
52 Fagalele
53 Leone
54 Amalula

55 Asili
56 Alao
57 Nua
58 Seetaga
59 Utumua
60 Agugulu
61 Fa'ilolo
62 Amanave
63 Poloa
64 Fagali'i
65 Maloata
66 Fagamalo
67 Aoloau Tuai
68 Aasu
69 Aoloau Fou
70 Mapusaga Fou

MANUA GROUP

TINI

Trailblazer in the wake of the Pitcairn

By

Abbie Le'ala Lam Yuen Watt

TEACH Services, Inc.
Brushton, New York

2000 01 02 03 04 05 06 07 08 09 · 5 4 3 2 1

The author assumes full responsibility for the accuracy
of all facts and quotations as cited in this book.

Copyright © 2000 TEACH Services, Inc.
ISBN 1-57258-166-2
Library of Congress Catalog Card No. 00-100619

Published by

TEACH Services, Inc.
254 Donovan Road
Brushton, New York 12916

Table of Contents

Dedication

This book is lovingly dedicated to my parents, Tini and Fuea, to my sisters and brothers, Florence, Puna, Man-Ha, Lam Yuen, Etenauga, Arthur, Tini Jr., Elaine and Hannacho, who shared in each experience, and to all the men and women who worked with Dad and Mom in presenting the three angels' messages into the islands and villages of Samoa.

Acknowledgments

Thank you Dad and Mom for a life of sacrifice and example.

I acknowledge with appreciation the guidance and endless help from my husband Jon, and my children Brandon, Jonathan, Shawn, and Michelle who periodically read original drafts, and especially Michelle for her creative illustrations and art work.

Also, thank you Mrs Alcyon Fleck for the pointers in writing, Dana Hulse for unbiased comments, Pr. David Hay — for your understanding inspiration, and Pulou Samana for enlightening information because you, too, shared in some of the challenging experiences.

Last but not least is heart-felt appreciation to Hans Voigt, who is an excellent interpreter and also keeper of original lists and records of the work in American Samoa, and my brother Lam for his countless and valued support.

Foreword

There's no doubt about the accomplishments of this trailblazer! Tini Inu Lam Yuen stands tall among God's pioneer missionaries. His remarkable record speaks for itself. Establishing and building up the presence of the Seventh-day Adventist church in American Samoa was no mean feat. Right from the beginning in 1946, until his transfer to Western Samoa in 1956, success marked his service.

In most instances the churches we have today throughout Tutuila and the outer islands can trace their beginnings to his influence. Tini's public evangelism and bible studies, executed with skill and enthusiasm, encouraged many truth-loving people, matai and taulealea, to establish a Seventh-day Adventist presence in their villages.

Even in Western Samoa, at Mission headquarters, with his added responsibilities of caring for personal ministries and Sabbath School for both Western and American Samoa, Tini's evangelistic fervor continued unabated. Assisted by members with a love for sharing Bible truth, he established new groups of believers on the southeast coast of Upolu. As he also desired a well-equipped membership for witnessing, he regularly trained interested members in Savaii, Upolu, and Tutuila for service in the villages.

Perhaps the spontaneous tributes spoken with love and sincerity at the 1991 'Pitcairn Centenary Celebration' gathering on Tutuila, best sum up the gratitude Seventh-day Adventists have for the long and faithful service of Pastor Tini Inu Lam Yuen. He was there. He heard them all. Although weakened by sickness, and finding movement difficult, there was no mistaking the shine in his eyes. Yes, he was well retired, but the flame of evangelism still burned brightly in his heart. It would always be there.

It was my privilege to personally associate with this man of God in Samoa for 17 years, and I'm pleased indeed his daughter, Leala, is recording his adventures for God. Having spent many hours listening to her father, and her mother Fuea recount the past, as well as remembering the many times she accompanied her parents on evangelistic journeys, she is well-equipped to accurately and warmly portray relevant events and people. My admiration is also for Tini's wife, Fuea. With her loving and loyal support, especially during times of trial, she has not only helped to keep his vision strong, but has also enriched his success.

David E Hay
President, Samoa Mission 1965–1974
President, Central Pacific Union Mission 1994–1995.

This fascinating account of one man's experiences is authentic and accurate. All activities, locations, and characters are real and true. This is the story of real people who devoted their lives in carrying Christ's mission.

I wish I could be more eloquent in writing this story, because it presents the message of love and guidance, of miracles and of success. More than that, it was triumph amongst disappointments and setbacks, and rewards after enduring trials. Most of all, it offers to inspire every reader who long to be a bearer of Christ's message. It is with deep respect and pride that I have attempted to honor all individuals involved in spreading the good news of God's love, in this corner of the vast South Pacific.

Tini (pronounced tee-nee) in Samoan means "the goal in a race" (noun), or "attaining a goal" (verb). Tini often said, even at a young age, that his life's goal was to save a soul. I believe he has led many people to Christ and has pointed many lives to the way of His salvation. As he retires from his ministry, I respectfully say that he is surely "tini."

Most of the experiences accounted here are familiar and in fact personal, therefore close to my heart. I grew up in the midst of these events. Tini Inu Lam Yuen is my very close friend, and he is my father.

The author

"How beautiful upon the mountains are the feet of those who bring good news,…who bring good tidings, who proclaim salvation…." (Isaiah 52:7, NIV)

Pastor and Mrs. Tini Lam Yuen
1989

Prologue:
A Spot In Paradise

As you read the story of a young missionary family and their experiences while introducing the gospel to an intensely devout Christian people, allow yourself to be an island-hopping traveler. First, imagine yourself on a boat leaving Apia, Western Samoa, with its shallow harbor littered with the wreckages of German, British, and American warships from a war for the possession of these islands. This war for domination ended with the great hurricane of 1889.

Western Samoa's total land area of 1130 square miles comprise the two main islands of Upolu and Savai'i, the twins Apolima and Manono, and five minor islets that flank this Rhode Island-size Pacific kingdom. The larger of the two Samoas with a population close to 150,000, Western Samoa, once under German control, became a British protectorate, then a New Zealand mandate under the United Nations Trusteeship Council, and now is an independent nation.

Tutuila, the largest and most known of the seven isles of American Samoa, is eighty sea miles to the east of Upolu. Pago Pago, the capital with its large land-locked harbor, is located on Tutuila. The other inhabited islands under the American flag include Ofu, Olosega, and Ta'u, known as the Manu'a group, and the tiny island of Aunu'u. The land mass of American Samoa totals close to seventy-eight square miles, and its population is approximately 52,000.

Scattered in the middle of the Pacific Ocean on a line between Hawaii and New Zealand, Samoa is 4400 sea miles southwest of San Francisco, and 1500 miles northeast of Auckland. It lies 14 degrees south of the Equator, with the international date line only minutes to the west. The annual rainfall is 125 inches, with an average temperature of 78 degrees, and humidity as high as 80 percent. Its tropical climate is tempered by the southeast trade winds which prevails throughout most of the year.

On these volcanic islands, tropical rain forests blanket most of the uncultivated land. A variety of tropical fruits and vegetables grow in abundance all year around. The patterns of land and use of the coast reflects the way of life and economy of each area. The Samoans have a deep love and respect for their land.

Agriculture is a principle occupation of the population on the larger islands of Western Samoa, exporting copra (dried coconut meat), cocoa, and bananas. In American Samoa, the land is mostly rough and mountainous. Two fish canneries, subsidiaries of large American companies, have provided jobs for many natives since the early 1950's.

Samoa is a land where the people proudly greet visitors in "fa'a-Samoa", the lifestyle of the Samoans, unchanged from their beginning. "Fa'a-Samoa" is characterized by the agricultural labors and fishing for their livelihoods, where everyone comes in contact with nature. This land, Samoa, is the home of the largest group of Polynesians in the Pacific.

The key to "fa'a-Samoa" is the "matai" (chief) system, the social order built on the "aiga" (extended family) and communal property. The extended family ("aiga") is the single focus of Samoan life. It may consist anywhere from a dozen to several hundred members, and its affairs are run by a "matai" (chief). No member of a family ever becomes poor or hungry; this would disgrace the "aiga".

To understand "fa'a-Samoa", one must also understand the role that religion plays within the people's lives. Before the missionaries came to the islands, each family member had his own god and "agaga" (spirit). The village chief or family head performed the priestly functions.

In the early 1830's, the "papalagi" (literally, heaven-bursters, but denotes a white man) John Williams, of the interdenominational London Missionary Society, arrived with his Christian message. Within a few years, most of the Samoans were converted to Christianity, and it remains a way of life today. In Western Samoa, the national motto— "Fa'avae i le Atua Samoa" ("Samoa is found on God")—attests religion's role in this society's existence.

Robert Louis Stevenson, the frail "Tusitala" ("writer of tales") from Scotland who went to Samoa for his health, humbly endeared himself to the native people, and became part of the legend of the South Seas. Arriving at Apia in 1889, Stevenson looked at the clear blue sea, the green hills that rose to the sky, and determined that here he had found his Paradise. He easily gained a knowledge and understanding of this warm, fun-loving people, as they regarded him with love and respect.

TINI

"**U**a sau le faife'au ("The minister is here.")," Mrs. Tini whispered to her husband. Then with more urgency in her voice, she repeated, "Ua sau le faife'au."

Tini peered up from behind the thick book he had been reading. The look on his face indicated that he did not hear the message. "Ua sau le faife'au," Mrs. Tini repeated for the third time.

The year was 1944. The young couple was not really surprised when the messenger arrived to summon them to town. "We have to go to Apia and hear what the committee has to say. There's been talk of some shifting around," Tini casually informed his wife.

At the Adventist Church headquarters in Apia, the executive committee had been meeting for days. The islands of American Samoa was the main subject of the discussion. In the middle of the previous year, a three-men research delegation, including Tini, was sent to Pago Pago to ascertain prospects of starting the work of the Adventist Church there. While in Pago Pago, the group visited the home of a Mr. and Mrs. George Bird. They had been well received and welcomed.

At the same time that the visitors landed on Tutuila, an Adventist American marine, named Sylvester Francisco, also arrived at the military base located on the island. On Sabbath, Francisco went in search of an Adventist Church to attend. He was unsuccessful; but in his search, the marine met the ministers from Apia.

"We desperately need to establish an Adventist work on this island," Francisco voiced his excitement. Later in the day, the marine approached the delegates. To show his sincerity, he handed a roll of money to the startled visitors. He explained, "And to help it get started, my friend and I would like to donate this first one hundred dollars."

When Tini and Fuea Lam Yuen arrived at the church headquarters in Apia, they were not surprised when the committee announced their new appointment. For the record, they were told, "You see, our work hasn't yet been introduced in the islands of American Samoa. This'll be a tremendous challenge to undertake." The statement was more or less a warning of what could be expected for their future.

The committee emphasized that Tini had relatives on Tutuila, which was an advantage. "They might possibly be helpful to our young family as they start their work," one member had pointed this in encouragement at an earlier meeting.

The challenge was overwhelming, and the decision was not an easy one to make. But without hesitation, the young family and all their belongings were soon sailing on the inter-island boat that took them to Pago Pago, the capital of American Samoa.

"We've prayed for guidance in everything that we do." Tini remembered how his little family often prayed and discussed mission work and missionary families. The course of their lives was set, and Tini thought reassuringly, "Now we'll do this work, and let God lead the way."

The journey took more than ten long hours, although it was not necessarily difficult or intolerable. Apia was now in the past. It was where Tini grew up and lived until this trip. Tini was the middle child in a family of five boys and one girl. Another sister had died in infancy.

When Tini was still young, he became a member of the Seventh-day Adventist Church. Ironically, Tini's first contact with the Adventist message came while he was a student at Marist Brothers', a Catholic school for boys, in Apia. His brothers also attended the same school. In one of his classes, the teacher, a highly educated friar had challenged the students with the Sabbath commandment. He asked the crucial question: "How was it kept, and why do you think it was changed, as it has been observed in modern times?" Thus, many questions were asked by the students who desperately wanted to understand, but most remained unanswered. Tini became curious, and he felt he needed to study these matters further.

From this point, Tini began to diligently study all the commandments and other Biblical subjects that challenged his way of thinking. His teacher became a great and invaluable friend. Tini was impressed by this educated Christian who

Pastor Tini, Fuea, and daughters Florence, Puna, and Man-Ha, leaving for American Samoa. 1944.

seemed well versed in the Scriptures. The friar became the sounding board whenever there were unanswered questions. In the end, this kind and patient teacher was instrumental in helping Tini towards his decision to follow the Bible truth.

After graduating at the top of his class, Tini attended Vailoa Missionary College, rather than accepting scholarship offers for further education at schools abroad. This Adventist boarding school was located on the far side of Upolu, some fifteen miles east of Apia. Tini's interest in scriptural and denominational doctrines grew, and he decided to concentrate his studies towards a ministerial career.

During the area-wide "Fono" (camp meeting) of 1935, Pastor A.G. Stewart from Australia visited the islands. When Pastor Stewart presented his challenge as to the role of the young people in God's work, Tini was impressed and very moved. He was only seventeen years old, but he became even more determined to fully dedicate his life to present this message. At the conclusion of the "Fono", Tini was baptized into the church by Pastor Raimond Reye, then president of the mission and a pioneering native missionary of Samoa.

Following his studies, Tini taught at one of the church's primary schools, in the village of Satomai. During this same time, he completed a year's ministerial internship under Pastor Sanika Afa'ese, a local minister and teacher.

In 1937, Tini was called to teach at Vailoa. Here he met and married Fuea, daughter of the village high chief, who had been raised by a Methodist minister. Presently, Fuea was attending Vailoa as a day student. Fuea's cousin, Pastor Neru Nu'uiali'i was one of the teachers.

Tini became the schoolmaster (principal) at Vailoa when the Second World War broke out, and some of the foreign missionaries had to return to their homelands. With Pastor John Howse, another pioneer from Australia, leading the work of the Samoa Mission, the educational system of the church began major reforms. Co-education was introduced to the boarding school, and he was put in charge of the young women's affairs. In addition Tini began organizing the work of the Junior Missionary Volunteers (JMV) club, which intensified and increased evangelism to the young people. The numbers in this age bracket had greatly multiplied in every church group throughout the islands of Western Samoa. Mr. Sauni Kuresa, the well-known and beloved native musician and composer of Samoa's national anthem, was called to assist with secretarial work in this newly created field.

Today, as the boat slowly eased alongside the wharf, Tini and Fuea, and their three young daughters gathered the few belongings they had carried with them on board. "This land's new and very different from what we're used to. But it's going to be good to us, and will be our home for a while," Tini tried to sooth the frightened children.

The family stood looking out over the crowd that had gathered to meet disembarking travelers, but they did not see any familiar faces. "God help us," Tini pleaded silently. Confidently, he directed his family to a waiting transporter. "Yes, we'll do all right, and God will help," Tini's voice brought smiles to the three faces looking up at him.

Enter The Adventists

Tini and his family were received at the home of Mrs. Ufanua Bird, a relative of Mr. Sauni Kuresa, the musician and youth leader, and a prominent member at the Apia church. Mrs. Bird was an Adventist Christian, but her husband, George, did not attend any particular church.

On their first Sabbath in Tutuila, Tini introduced the advent message of the Book of Revelation to his small congregation, and to American Samoa. "Jesus is coming soon. We must work hard and thorough to spread this message." There were tears in Tini's eyes as he spoke of the challenge ahead.

In this land where the London Missionary Society first brought the Christian gospel more than a hundred years earlier, there seemed to be many obvious obstacles already. The Adventist Church had arrived on American Samoa, and God's workers prayed for courage to remain ready and fit to undertake any challenges.

After staying at Mrs. Bird's home for several weeks, Tini moved his family to Taputimu, a village at the west end of Tutuila. "You've been a great friend; you've treated us as part of your family." Tini's family appreciated this kindness, and for the greater part of this year, the two families remained closely associated.

On first priority, Tini and Mrs. Bird discussed the evangelistic strategy for the months ahead. "On the weekdays, I'll need to stay around here, while I work among the townspeople. Then I can also distribute literature to the villagers along the eastern half of the island." Tini expressed his excitement because of the reception he had received from the public so far.

Tini going out to distribute the "Tala Moni." 1946 to 1947.

For almost a year, Sabbath services were held at the home of this gracious family. On the weekends, Tini's family would return to town to worship with the group. During these first ten months, Tini distributed the "TALA MONI" ("The True Word") as it arrived by boat from Apia. He traveled the length of the island by bicycle, the only available mode of transportation.

The battles of the great war (World War II) was at its fiercest at this time. During these first tense years, the "TALA MONI", the only church circular in the Samoan language, film strips and other religious supplies were under wartime restrictions and censorship. Quite often, it took a number of weeks for the responsible government official to view and examine the contents. Then the official decision would determine whether the material was appropriate for the public. Some of the materials were never returned.

Tutuila's main road follows the coastline, and the only vehicles during these war years belonged to the United States military. At this time, American Samoa was serving as the supply base for equipment and military servicemen in the Pacific war front.

The government provided and operated two buses for general public transportation. Each bus traveled daily to the opposite ends of Tutuila, then returned to town with passengers, who often did not return home until the next day's trip. Most of the traveling in the islands was done by foot, canoe, or by bicycle, a rare luxury at the time.

Within a few months, the Adventist message had swept through the entire length of Tutuila, from Tula in the east to Poloa at the extreme west, where the road ended. In the remaining years of the decade following the end of the war, literature distribution intensified, and it became a very powerful and important evangelistic tool indeed. Over four hundred subscribers were receiving the "TALA MONI". In addition, evangelistic meetings and Bible studies throughout the villages of Tutuila continued to multiply and flourish on a steady cycle. Miraculously, to this point all mission work and activities had cost very little financially to the church.

Since their arrival on Tutuila, Tini had been searching around the island for a piece of land to build a church and establish a mission compound. However, land for sale was scarce, and the citizens were hesitant to associate with the "thin young preacher," as Tini was now known, and his unique message. Traditionally, land is familial property that is handed down to generations through inheritance.

By the end of the tenth month, a half-acre lot was obtained at Satala, a suburban village on the periphery of town. This fortune was made possible through a lease agreement made with Mrs. B. F. Kneubahl ("Lina"), the wife of a businessman well respected and established on American Samoa. With much faith in God's guidance, Tini accepted the terms of the lease, which was offered to the church at sixty dollars (U.S. $60) a year. This was indeed a very reasonable price for prime land in a prime location.

A lay worker named Pasi promptly volunteered and was sent from Apia to assist in the building program. Tini and Pasi immediately started the work by cutting timber from a forest on the western end of Tutuila. A government-owned truck was acquired to transport the wood to Satala. Thatch ("lau") for the roof was obtained from a considerate neighbor.

Mission: Completed

"L au" (thatch) is made from "launiu" (coconut fronds) or "lautolo" (sugar cane leaves) woven tightly together. A supply of these materials had to be obtained before any building could be completed. Adjacent to the new building site at Satala was the land belonging to Papu Siofele, a teacher in the public schools system. On his land there was an abundance of coconut palm trees.

Tini believed that God had surely guided him to this part of the land. He decided to ask Papu for materials for the thatch. One late Sabbath afternoon, Tini and Pasi went to visit Papu's family.

After the introductions, Tini simply stated, "We're new in Tutuila. But my family and our guest are here for our church." Papu nodded in acknowledgment, but did not seem moved. Tini continued quickly, "We'd like to begin the work on our home and church building soon, which'll be adjacent to your property." Then matter-of-factly, Tini made his request. "We have our lumber, but need thatch for the roof. Would you be willing to sell us the material from your coconut plantation? (This way the trees would produce more when the fronds have been thinned out.)."

The visitors answered a few personal questions for a short while longer. They felt their reception by this family was personable and warm, so they expressed their appreciation, and indicated further interests. Tini and Pasi then returned home to pray for a positive reply from Papu.

On the following day, the two men visited Papu and his family again. They found the family seated for their Sunday dinner. Papu and a few friends were drinking beer and in the middle of a heated discussion. He left the table when the men approached. To Tini's request, Papu was generous.

The first "falelotu", (church and parsonage) in Satala, American Samoa. 1946.

"Cut whatever you require. And any other help you need, please feel free to ask." Papu was very courteous and friendly to the strangers. He did not realize yet, that this first contact would set the stage for the change that was soon to happen in his life.

On the other hand, Mrs. Siofele was angry that these strangers had dared to come around and worked on her property on her Sabbath. "This is the worst crime," she had told her husband. Although she was angry, Mrs. Siofele was patient. She wanted only to impress her new neighbors.

The work to gather leaves and prepare the thatch proved tedious and time consuming. It dragged on for several Sundays. In the meantime, Papu realized that his wife's patience was running dry, and it was becoming harder to control her anger. Papu decided to help the neighbors complete their work quickly, so he gave them roofing materials he had prepared for his own house. The mission building was usable a few days later.

Pasi returned to Western Samoa after one year of helping to establish the mission compound at Satala.

In May of 1945, Tini relocated his family to the almost completed new "fale lotu" (mission house). It took many trips to move the family's belongings from Taputimu to Satala, but it proved to be a critical blow to Mrs. Siofele. She watched silently but inwardly she was mocking the strange Sunday workers. "I wonder what kind of God they worship, and why is it so important for them to worship on Saturday?"

Soon, the Sabbath worshipers settled into a peculiar routine. On Saturdays, Tini and his family moved all their belongings outdoors and to one corner of the house, then the building was prepared for the church services. After sunset, everything was moved back into place in the house. Thus was the tiresome weekend routine in Tini's household for a seemingly long time, and regardless of the type of weather.

Although the site of the new "falesa" (church) bothered Mrs. Siofele, she was also becoming curious. One Sabbath morning a few weeks later, Papu and his two young sons, Joe and Willie visited the meetings. The trio promptly returned home after the church service. There were no exchanges or conversations. But to Papu's dismay, while he was at church his wife took all his clothes and threw them out of the house, after she had cut them into shreds.

"Are you in your right mind, visiting those crazy meetings?" she asked her husband sarcastically. She was furious, but also embarrassed that her husband was becoming acquainted with the strange new neighbors. "I'm going to see that we won't be influenced by such nonsense." Mrs. Siofele vowed quietly, as she was determined to end this involvement.

As for Papu, the challenge was yet to come. His interest in the Adventist message increased with every Bible study he attended. However, the devil was also working hard to create setbacks and diversions. Presently, Mrs. Siofele was expecting a child in June. To avoid further complications for the time being, Papu decided to keep his distance from the church temporarily.

Following the birth of their daughter, Papu was even more determined to follow the Biblical truth he had learned. The first Saturday after mother and baby were home from the hospital proved to be a memorable one, and the turning point in this family's life.

On Friday evening , Tini gathered his family for their sundown worship. Aware of the familiar routine at the mission, Mrs. Siofele took her baby and settled at a cottage within hearing distance of the service at the neighbor's. When the singing started, Mrs. Siofele decided to return to their main house, but intentionally walking within clear view of the worshipers.

Mrs. Tini had on several occasions tried to visit her neighbor, but had been unsuccessful. Now she saw the opportunity before her this time, so she went out and invited her neighbor to the service. "You're kind, and we're not busy at the moment," Mrs. Siofele seemed to be a changed person, and she quickly accepted the invitation. Excitedly, she sent for her husband, who was pleasantly surprised, and sons to join the group.

Tini and Papu Siofele after first baptism at Satala. 1946.

This occasion was the turning point for the Adventist work, which so far had barely made a mark in American Samoa. It was also the beginning of a new life-style for the Siofele family. Papu's beer-drinking with friends had ceased after he started attending church on the Sabbath.

Following vespers and the evening meal, the group learned new songs and hymns. As the group separated for the evening, Mrs. Siofele felt an unusual eagerness for the following day.

Very early the next morning, Papu arose at about two o'clock, to prepare his family's meals for the day. He and his sons wanted to leave for the services early. He had carefully avoided mentioning to his wife any of his plans for the Sabbath day. Silently he had prayed to God, "May this be the fulfillment of my new hope. I have faith in Your direction."

While the three were preparing to leave the house, Mrs. Siofele casually strolled out the door ahead of them without saying a word, her baby and bag in hand. Outside of the house, she simply stated, "We decided to join the group for church."

"Thank you Lord for these blessings," Papu whispered as he watched his family walk ahead of him towards the service. He felt relieved, and a new sense of freedom almost overcame him to tears.

In Sabbath School, the subject of the lesson study was appropriately, "The Sabbath-Seal of God, and Sunday — the Mark of the Beast?"

"I never knew, and I didn't think anything like this was in the Bible." Mrs. Siofele later told how these lessons disturbed but fascinated her.

For the sermon, Tini presented Christ's challenge to His followers: "I gave all for you; what have you done for Me?"

As for Mrs. Siofele, there was no more doubt in her mind about the truth. It had always been in her Bible, but she had not realized it. She got to her feet, and with tears in her eyes she gave her heart-felt testimony and acknowledged her newly found understanding of the Scriptures. "I despised these people, and mocked the strange message they were preaching about the Sabbath." She emphasized the skepticism she felt, because no one could have known the Scriptures better than her devoutly Christian parents. Her parents had taught her everything that was important to know in the Bible, from a very young age. But as she understood differently, her heart was touched.

As the new year, 1946, came under way, Papu Siofele and his wife, along with four others were baptized. They became the earliest charter members of the newly organized Seventh-day Adventist Church on American Samoa. Pastor H.B. Christian, then President of the Samoa Mission, officiated on this joyous occasion.

A short time later, Siofele's family joined the church's work force and were transferred to Western Samoa, where Papu taught in church schools for several years. Later he was ordained to the ministry, pastoring churches in different districts of both Western and American Samoa, until he retired in the early 1970's.

Following his retirement, Pastor and Mrs. Siofele moved to America where some of the children had settled with their own families in California. After a long illness, dear Mrs. Siofele passed away in 1990.

The workers of the Samoa Mission, Australasian Division, at the dedication of Apia Central Church. 1947.

On Faith, Blessings, A Typhoid Epidemic

One of Tini's first visits when he arrived on Tutuila was to the village of Vaitogi, famous for its legend of the "Laumei ma le Malie" (turtle and the shark). He had collected enough film strips to conduct his "malamalama" service (evangelistic meeting with films shown). Tini and Fuea were received at the home of Chief John Ufuti. He and his family were immediately impressed that the "faife'au Aso Fitu" (Adventist minister) had been directed to them by the Holy Spirit.

"We're convinced God led you to our family, because we've been searching for more than what we already know," Ufuti expressed his eagerness for a more positive view of God.

"This is only the beginning of God's good news," Tini explained to the couple. "The whole Bible is the story of God's love," he simply added.

The evangelistic meetings continued at this village for several months and ended with a few being baptized, including John and his wife. However, not all was well with the rest of the villagers and the chiefs. Soon Ufuti and his family were threatened with expulsion from the village. A message was sent to Ufuti. "The village council has met and agreed on punishment," Ufuti was told one evening. "If you don't conform to the village wish, you'll be expelled and your lands and properties forfeited to the village."

Impressed by Tini's soft, straight-forward answer to maintain his faith, Ufuti refused to reply in anger against those who tried to discourage him. He thought for a while, then went to seek out Tini. "My family and I have prayed for an answer to our difficulty," Ufuti told Tini simply, his low voice betraying his sadness. "I think it'll be best that we leave our home, even our country." For a moment, Ufuti appeared lost in thought. Then with determination in his eyes, he announced, "We're going to America!"

Ufuti's family left Samoa for the United States shortly thereaf-

Adults and children of the early church, American Samoa. 1947.

ter, where they settled on the island of Oahu, Hawaii. Soon, Ufuti the exile began to tell families, friends, and neighbors in their new homeland about God's love. He organized a congregation of fellow Samoans and met as a church company in the rural town of Nanakuli.

Chief Ufuti and his family remained in Hawaii for several years. In time they moved again and settled in Southern California, around the city of Oceanside. Again they began to tell friends, neighbors and family members in the area about God's great plan of salvation, a message dear to his heart. And once again, Ufuti organized his fellow believers and established the congregation which became the Samoan Seventh-day Adventist Church in Vista, California.

In the meantime, God's spirit had moved on those other villagers and families who had attended the "malamalama" (meetings) with Ufuti. In time they too accepted God's message, and by the year 1956, at least five "matais" (chiefs) and their families from the village of Vaitogi had been baptized. Tini had persisted in nurturing the seeds that had been planted a few years before.

When Ufuti and his grown family returned to Samoa years later, he proceeded to deed much of his land to the church and to build a "fale sa" (church building). "It's true that God can build a mountain from nothing. But it only happens when we have faith," Ufuti chuckled, and Tini understood what his friend was referring to.

Towards the middle of the year, Tini had to travel to Apia on church business. However, Tini returned to Tutuila after a few days, when he received news of his daughter's illness. When he returned, he spent his days at the hospital with Florence. In the late afternoons, he traveled by bicycle to Satala, where he was holding evangelistic meetings in the evenings. Following the services Tini returned to the hospital where he spent the rest of the night.

These difficulties became challenges to Tini. And to him challenges presented opportunities and blessings. Sick at the hospital together with Florence was a man named Lokeni. He had been critically ill with typhoid fever for several days, and his wife remained at his bedside. While Tini maintained his vigil at Florence's bedside, he kept a routine of starting and ending the day with a prayer for all those who were suffering. More than that, he prayed for the families who were going through the same pain as he was for his daughter.

In spite of his condition, Lokeni was impressed with this simple young man and his faith. "Would it be possible to give us Bible studies here and now?" Lokeni whispered to Tini one day. From his sickbed, he requested if Tini would explain the gospel message to himself and his wife.

"Yes, and God will help us study to understand His word, here and now," Tini reassured Lokeni.

Lokeni remained in the hospital for seven months, as he recovered from his near-fatal experience. And for seven months, Tini held Bible studies for this couple. Lokeni vowed that when he went home from the hospital, he and his family would be baptized. This faithful couple began honoring the Sabbath commandment the day they learned about its truth.

As soon as Lokeni went home to his family and village of Nu'uuli, he started a branch Sabbath School. Unfortunately, the only time available for Tini to start the new service was Sunday morning. So for Lokeni's family, if they were able, they traveled to Satala for Sabbath services. On Sunday morning they held Sabbath School for Nu'uuli members until Tini was able to conduct Saturday services a few months later.

The village of Malaeloa was the next challenge for Tini. A man named Palafu and his family had attended evangelistic meetings at Satala, a short distance from where they lived at the village of Pago Pago. Palafu's elderly mother had joined the family at the meetings, and at the conclusion the three adults were baptized.

Upon their return home, Palafu and his newly baptized family were told that they had no place in this village. "You've disgraced our family's name before the village," the furious "matai" (chief) lashed out at the members. "You'll do well to leave here and never return."

Quietly, Palafu and his family returned to the church compound that same evening. There they were welcomed as part of Tini's growing family, for more than two months. Ironically, at the end of this time the same "matai" (chief) sent a messenger requesting Palafu to return to the village.

Palafu did not hesitate and chose to face his "matai". "I've decided I'll not go back nor have my family around this part of the clan again," Palafu told the chief when he politely declined his offer. "This time, I'd like to return to my father's village of Malaeloa. I've a message of hope to share with this part of my clan." With those thoughts, Palafu left his mother's village and began a venture that would last the rest of his life.

"Do you think my faith is strong enough to sustain us in the difficult times ahead?" Palafu asked Tini directly as he discussed his plans.

Tini was impressed with this simple man's determination. With a kind and reassuring voice, he answered, "God will always sustain you, if you put your faith in Him." As for his plans Tini told Palafu that he was a noble person with solid goals.

As soon as Palafu was settled in Malaeloa, complications started as the devil sought to block any spread of the gospel to this end of Tutuila. Persecutions began as the family sustained harassments constantly. At the end the village, the clan, and the

Baptized adults of American Samoa company with Pastor and Mrs. H.B. Christian, mission President. 1947.

"matai" (chief) went to the civil court and filed a complaint against Palafu and his family, claiming there was interference of village affairs by the presence of this Adventist family. When the unpleasant event was over, Palafu was granted the right to bring his church to Malaeloa, and he was free to worship in any way he wanted. Palafu was convinced that God always won when affairs of men seek to hamper His work.

A short distance from the village of Vaitogi was Futiga, located on a high bluff above a sandy peninsula known as Fagatele. While Tini was working extensively with the members at Vaitogi and Malaeloa, he contacted a prominent "matai" (chief) from Futiga, who owned prime property in several villages on this west side of Tutuila. Aumavae was a lay preacher in a Christian church.

From the start, Tini was well received by this Christian family. He was invited to conduct his "malamalama" (evangelistic service) at their home. A few Sabbaths later, Tini and Fuea arrived at Fagatele to find a large crowd of the "aiga" (extended family). Among them were Aumavae's two sisters, one sister's husband, and their families. They were eager to study the Sabbath School lesson.

After two Sabbaths of hiking over rough trails, the two sisters boldly presented their request to Tini. "We can't keep coming down to this isolated place, 'lau Susuga Tini' (an honored title)," one sister pleaded. "Please come up to Futiga where the rest of us live."

Aumavae was delighted with his "aiga's" (family) response to the gospel message. The congregation grew so rapidly that this thoughtful "matai" again moved his group to yet another family land, and there he built a "fale lotu" (church house). This was the year 1947. More than a decade later, Aumavae and his sisters donated several acres of prime family land at the village of Iliili, known as Iakina, to the church they had grown to love. Ili'ili was the fourth company to organize on Tutuila. Here, at last, the headquarters for the American Samoa district of the Samoa Mission of Seventh-day Adventists was relocated in 1979.

Operation Evangelism

From the beginning, Tini conducted individualized studies and Bible discussion groups to introduce the advent message in different villages. He utilized every means available to communicate with people of upcoming services. And he tried to utilize all tools of evangelism that were available to him. Tini was well received, and his message began to stir the minds of many. There were those who were curious, but most were looking for answers. Tini was able to draw people of all ages and with different religious backgrounds.

During the first series of meetings in Satala, many members of the Church of Latter-day Saints from the community and the outlying villages visited the services. They were impressed with the message as they heard it. After one particular meeting, some of these members went and sought out one of their church leaders, who was well-versed in their doctrines.

"We've found a very exciting way to study the Scriptures. It has given us a new understanding of Jesus and His teachings." The members commented to their leader, with an enthusiasm that mirrored the uplifting renewal of their spiritual experience. They all seemed sincere in their search for Biblical truth. The group thus invited the leader to attend the following meeting with them.

The leader graciously accepted the invitation, and attended the very next day. From the start, the man felt repulsed by some information presented. He often interrupted the discussion with questions. Like a raging storm, he bombarded Tini with comments and questions, whether they were relevant to the subject or not. However, Tini calmly answered, with Scriptural references, all his inquiries.

As a result of these meetings, many of the brothers and sisters present turned to the truth and were baptized as Christ's followers. Among this group were Atimani, Eli and his wife, Ta'a and Taufao, Falefatu Utu and others. Slowly, the "falelotu" (mission house) began to fill up on Sabbath.

Along with such successes were moments of discouragement and setbacks. Basic materials for everyday needs and for survival, such as food, medicine, hygienic items, and even clean water, became scarce at times. During such times, and under these conditions, the devil seemed to work his best and hardest to prevent the truth from spreading.

One of the biggest difficulties was transportation. For most of the population, transportation around the islands was largely by foot. However, the word was spreading fast about the Adventist meetings. Homes scattered in distant villages were opened up, and requests began arriving for new meetings and study groups. In response, services were held simultaneously in several villages to try and fulfill all requests. Such was the case of Vatia and Fagamalo, two villages on the north shore's "backside" of Tutuila. The only roads leading to these people were narrow trails over rugged vertical terrain.

Grandma Lam Yuen with Rose Leutu Alai (McNeave), first registered nurse from American Samoa, after her baptism. 1949.

These narrow trails were often obscured by brush, because they were seldom traveled and because they traversed heavy rain forests. It often required hours of hiking before reaching a village. And for the meetings, Tini had to carry backpacked all the needed equipment. This included the "malamalama" (term denoting projector and carbide battery to run it, slides and film strips), books and literature, and sometimes clothing and bedding for extended visits. Then on some occasions, daughters Florence and Puna, ten and eight years old, went along to help their father with the service. On such days, Tini preached the sermon and the girls provided the music and help with the young people.

As the church grew and the members were being baptized from throughout the island of Tutuila, "companies" and branch Sabbath Schools were organized in several of the villages. These included Nu'uuli, Vaitogi, Ili'ili, Malaeloa, and Leone to the west, and Alao and Masefau in the east. Satala became the headquarters for the American Samoa district. Tini maintained consistant communication and conducted services and studies at each of the established locations.

At the height of this series, two lay workers, Uta and Pasi, and their families arrived from Western Samoa, to help Tini as the work progressed rapidly. Their assistance was much appreciated during this stage of growth in the ministry. More evangelistic meetings and Bible studies were started, and many more new members joined the church.

An outstanding and refreshing experience occurred from these beginnings at Afono, a particularly difficult village to penetrate on Tutuila's north shore. Afono was isolated by its mountainous location and was hardly accessible through the single rugged foot path.

Tafeaga and his wife, Siniva, were members of the Satala church, where Tafeaga was its very first head elder. One day, Siniva suffered a severe debilitating stroke and remained gravely ill for some time. Believing that she was not going to improve, and the hospital could no longer help her, the family transferred Siniva to Afono, her home village, to die.

The elderly mother continued in this critical condition for several weeks. And every Sabbath following the services at Satala, Tini traveled to Afono to visit the sick member. Soon, Tini had to leave Tutuila for Apia to attend the week long annual session for the church's leaders. Hans Voigt, a young lay worker and a member from Satala, was appointed to continue the spiritual ministerings for the ailing mother.

On the Sabbath after he returned from Apia, Tini conducted communion at Satala. Then following this special inspirational meeting, he and several other church members traveled to Afono to minister and offer communion on

First "falesa", (church building) after organization of American Samoa church. 1951.

behalf of Siniva. During the emotional service, Tini was touched by the power of faith and the strength such as displayed by all those present. A special prayer session ended the day, and Tini's visiting party returned to Satala.

Early on Monday, Tini was surprised by the sudden appearance of Tafeaga, Siniva's husband. Excitedly, he informed Tini of the miraculous turn of events. "It was as if a refreshing shower landed on Siniva after you and the group left two days ago," Tafeaga spoke as if each word was being measured. "After you left on Sabbath, Siniva began asking for food and drink. During the night she had a restful and painless sleep. And that, I know, she hasn't had since before she got sick." Tears began to cloud the old man's eyes, but he continued, "By Sunday morning, my wife was able to stand and move about. Her legs that had been weak and numb seemed to be slowly healing."

Tini remained speechless as Tafeaga related his family's weekend experience. He could only agree with the elder, and together they uttered prayers of thanksgiving to God. "We must never doubt the power of healing, especially if the Lord has plans for our lives," Tini reminded Tafeaga of God's promise.

Siniva fully recovered in record time, and she remained a very active church member till she died of natural causes, more than twelve years later. Siniva was in her early eighties. This sister's life and testimony was strong assurance to God's people, that His work would always move forward despite human setbacks.

By now, Tini was able to purchase a surplus military jeep. Transportation to areas where there was a road improved greatly. However, the long hikes and backpacking continued, when meetings were held in villages without roads. Often, the evangelistic team was exhausted by the time they reached their destination.

For several years, Tini continued his multiple services routine, and the church membership continued to increase. The strong help of the lay workers was another assurance that God was leading the work in this island group. Furthermore, the lives of the young people was a positive influence for God's work.

The other branch churches were located in villages scattered throughout the western end of Tutuila. Occasionally, joint Sabbath services held at the mission compound brought all the members together for worship. For these joint meetings, Tini went out early on Sabbath morning, and transported members from villages on all sides of the island. On these instances, the vehicle with the capacity of six carried as many as fourteen people on each trip. Only a few members were able to find their own transportation, while some had to walk long distances to get there on time for the services.

In this way, Tini brought all the members to the compound in seven or eight trips. There they anxiously awaited the "lali call", announcing the beginning of Sabbath School at nine o'clock. After the evening vespers, Tini resumed his "bus service" to return everyone to their respective homes.

Later on many occasions, the members extended these meetings so that everyone from various distances began gathering at Satala on Friday evening. Most were able to stay until Sunday, making for each a rewarding experience in fellowship with faith and sharing with each other.

"We Are A Missionary Band"

As the church on Tutuila grew, Tini continued to utilize all available resources to help in his work. His young family also grew in size, and Tini and Fuea realized with delight the resourcefulness of these young lives they were blessed with.

To Florence and Puna, the numerous trips and moves, first from island to island then between villages, that the family made were to do God's work. The girls were barely seven and five years old when their mission adventure began. Tini had been involved with Bible studies and "malamalama" (evangelistic meetings) in the villages on the north side of Tutuila. Transportation to these villages was limited to trekking over the mountain range through a heavy rainforest.

"Florence, you'll need to carry our hymn book and some 'Tala Moni' (church magazine)," Tini instructed his oldest daughter as they prepared for the journey. Then lifting his second daughter on his lap, Tini smiled and said, "And you, little Puna, can carry your change of clothes."

Tini and Fuea had spoken to the girls of the long walk up the hill and then down to the beautiful village on the beach at the other side. "Papa, will there be lots of children in this village when we get there?" Puna asked Tini quietly, her yawns indicating it was almost bedtime for them.

"We'll be meeting with some people you've never seen before, and they have children," Tini whispered into Puna's ear. Seeing the confusion in her sleepy eyes, her father continued, "We'll tell Bible stories and teach them some nice songs that you both know." Tini assured the girls as he hugged them to him.

Puna's eyes lighted up with the mention of songs. Around the house she was always singing or making up songs.

A baptism shortly after the dedication of the new church building. 1951.

Florence, on the other hand was always asking questions. She would ask out of curiosity, but mainly she always wanted to understand.

"Why do we need to teach people about the Sabbath?" Florence asked Tini one day. Then she commented, "I'm very happy we go to our 'Lotu Aso Fitu' (Seventh-day Adventist Church), Papa."

By the year 1947, Tini had launched his ministry for the young people, organizing the Junior Missionary Volunteer and Missionary Volunteers clubs (JMV and MV). The JMV meetings were held on one or two weekdays, while the MV service was on Sabbath afternoons. Florence and Puna, and later the other children were instrumental in maintaining this successful evangelism.

At this time a young government contract worker from Western Samoa arrived on Tutuila. Hans Voigt had been active in the young people's organization at his home church in Apia. Tini immediately found in Hans a great and valuable leader for this work. Later he became a resourceful and dependable leader as a deacon then an elder, as well as serving in various 'er capacities for the church he loved.

Chapter 6

Towards the end of the decade, more villages on the north shores of Tutuila became involved in Bible studies. Tini's trips to these difficult outreach increased. And Puna became his main companion on these travels. She was a light-hearted, easy-going and self-sufficient traveler. Florence was a welcome help for Fuea at home with the rest of the family.

The young people and number of children at the Sabbath meetings in Satala were increasing. And they learned to sing "We are a missionary band..." as they became involved in Sabbath afternoon activities. These included literature distribution and Bible studies.

Tini was ordained as a minister of the gospel in 1947, after he had been at work in American Samoa for several years.

Over The Mountain And Beyond

Masefau, a village on the north shore of Tutuila was accessible only by a twisted foot path. While Tini had been occupied with Bible studies for Lokeni at the hospital and evangelistic meetings in the evenings at Satala, on Sabbaths he spent the afternoon at Masefau. Tini and Fuea, or the older daughters traveled this difficult trail after the services at Satala.

Because Masefau was on the back side of the mountain, Tini drove his jeep to the village at the base where he left it with a kind family until his return. The two to three hour hike up the mountain was tedious and difficult. However, even unpleasant weather was never a hindrance for Tini or his scheduled meetings. At Masefau, members of two large prominent families accepted the advent message.

At the home of the elderly Eli, an informal Bible study drew several curious neighbors. One Sabbath, the little "fale tele" (family council house) was full of new faces. One newcomer with a scowl on his face had a muscular frame of a strong body builder. Tini sensed an air of power and strength that matched the booming voice when the man spoke.

Eliapo, recently paroled from prison, wanted to know about the tall, skinny "faife'au Aso Fitu" (Adventist minister) who seemed to be disturbing this peaceful mountain neighborhood. He had served a term for a killing committed under provocation, but now was confronted by such powerful yet unfamiliar teachings. Eliapo was curious because he had never heard of this church or its message. To Tini, the man seemed anxious to battle against anyone who discounted his own h beliefs.

Throughout the lesson study, Eliapo was gracious in his enquiries. As if they were the only two people in the study, Tini presented the Scriptures in answer to all Eliapo's questions on faith, conversion and forgiveness. This

When Florence, oldest daughter was baptized at Satala. 1952.

powerfully built man explained at length his dissatisfaction with his life, and that he was resigned to the fact that he was forever lost because of his sin. "I killed a man and my minister expressed damnation as my ending," he stated dejectedly.

Slowly Tini explained Jesus' sacrifice on the cross and the plan of salvation. "God's plan is for every one of us," Tini assured Eliapo, whose booming voice no longer sounded threatening. "Our only part is to accept Him."

Eliapo was impressed by the simple message of a forgiving God. From this very first meeting, this violent-tempered, troubled man pledged his whole life and soul to God. "I sincerely believe God led me to this extraordinary study," he testified at the end of the service. "I vowed to the law authorities that my life was changed by my time in prison. Now I know that Jesus is the real One that changed my life and He set me free."

As the study sessions drew to a close, the members requested that the meetings be extended. "Do you think we may be able to continue to meet as a branch Sabbath School?" the group timidly asked Tini after services one day.

"'Lau Susuga Tini' (honored title), I'd be honored if we hold the services at my house next Sabbath," Eliapo boldly requested when he approached the leader. Tini gladly agreed.

Eliapo and his family dutifully prepared for this occasion. When Tini and his wife arrived on Sabbath afternoon, the "fale" (open house) was filled with anxious smiling faces. Even this make-shift "fale sa" (worship house) had been rearranged for the church service, complete with a table for the pulpit and rows of "fala" (mats) for the congregation.

From this simple beginning, the church at Masefau continued to meet at this location for years to come. On some occasions, the group from Masefau joined with all the members from Tutuila as they gathered for special Sabbath services. At Satala, Tini conducted communion, baptisms, or services for visiting church dignitaries. For many years, Tini provided the mode of transportation for the members.

Eliapo devised creative means to transport his growing family from the mountain-top village to the road. He carried in woven baskets with a yoke over his shoulders the two younger children who could not descend the mountain safely. The four older ones carried the loads of clean clothes and food supplies for the day.

Within a few weeks, regular Sabbath services were conducted at the village of Masefau. Eli, his wife and several other family members, and Eliapo, his wife and children accepted the advent message and were baptized into the church. With these influential members, a strong base was formed for the Adventist work in this part of Tutuila, American Samoa.

Eliapo and his family remained true messengers for the work of God. And when most of the grown family immigrated to the San Francisco area in the early seventies, they continued to work and spread the gospel to those they come in contact with. Masefau has been one of the favorite sites for youth retreats. It is still a fair hike to the campsite; however, a two-way road now winds its way to the village.

Unlike Masefau, Leone is a large, sprawling village on the western end of Tutuila. By the year 1950, two organized branch Sabbath Schools were already established on the eastern end, so Tini returned to concentrate his work in the more populated western end of the island. At Leone, he paid a visit at the home 'ulou Samana and his family.

lou and his wife had been studying the Scriptures with ung evangelists from a popular religion. On the day of

Tini's visit, the "faife'au papalagi" (foreign ministers) were also there. At first, the two men were excited that the newcomer expressed interest and seemed eager to join in the study. "And who is our new visitor?" they asked Pulou.

"Tini is the "faife'au Aso Fitu" (Adventist minister) on Tutuila," Pulou replied simply. Sometime later, Pulou told Tini that his visit on this particular day was God-sent in answer to his prayer.

As Tini graciously accepted the invitation to participate in the study, the evangelists quickly emphasized, "You can learn a lot of good things about the Bible that you probably don't know."

Baptism of Mr. and Mrs. Pulou Samana. 1953.

From the start, the two "faife'au" (ministers) challenged the validity of the seventh-day Sabbath. "Why are the Adventists still keeping this Old Testament day of rest?" the men blatantly asked Tini, arrogance shown in their tone. "We've done extensive studies on the subject, and there's no way we're wrong," they claimed.

Unknown to the evangelists, this subject of the seventh-day Sabbath was the challenge that reigned in Tini's life. He considered it a very essential factor in the Christian's walk with God, and he too had studied it extensively. The educated visitors maintained that the New Testament was the valid part of the Scriptures for our day, while Tini persistently made references to the whole Bible.

"What makes us think we can decide on which part of the Bible to honor or which to discount?" Tini finally commented to the two men. "Personally, I'd be afraid to be selective on which is applicable or which is not, in case I miss something." He eyed the men to check for reaction, but there wasn't any. Smiling, he continued, "I guess what I'm saying is God's word should always be considered current."

Towards the end of the morning, Pulou noticed that the discussion was mostly one-sided by now. Most of the questions Tini presented remained unanswered. The young evangelists seemed frustrated when Tini consistently emphasized the Scriptures over their own religious sources.

"We must be able to explain and prove Scripture with Scripture," Tini finally concluded. "No source outside His Word can ever explain the plan God designed for the salvation of mankind. That include each of us." Tini's last words were spoken slowly and gently, as if to try and sooth their frustrated stares.

After the three visitors left, Mrs. Pulou approached her husband with a request. She had been a silent but very attentive spectator during the Bible discussion. "You and I have been searching for a church that believe and teach from the Bible, and Tini has been doing exactly that," Mrs. Pulou stressed to her husband. "Now I'm convinced Tini was directed to us so we may follow in the teachings that lead us to Christ rather than to a destructive ending. Let's ask for some "malamalama" (evangelistic meetings) here in our compound."

Tini returned to Leone in a few days and announced that the request was gladly accepted. Preparations were made and within a few weeks evening meetings and Sabbath services commenced at Pulou's "fale tele" (great family dwelling). By the end of the year, a modest "fale sa" (house of worship) was erected and designated for Leone Church services on Pulou's family land. In addition to Pulou, his wife and children, four other prominent families had joined as original members of this congregation. These included the families of Talalelei, Fa'atiu, Fa'apepele and others. But Leone's membership grew so fast that a larger "fale lotu" (church building) was added to the compound.

Through the years, Leone has gone through several building phases, each one larger than the last. When Tini began the Adventist work on the islands of Manu'a, he called on Pulou to ๖mpany him. This was the beginning of Pulou's service for ๐rd and His church. He and his wife have remained faith-ᶟnesses wherever they traveled or resided.

Setbacks And Mrs. Tini

By late 1946, the church was able to purchase an acre and a half parcel of prime land from Norman Foster, a property owner who lived next to the mission compound in Satala. This land was rich with breadfruit trees, its fruit a major dietary staple on the islands. A sizable taro and banana plantation was soon added.

At times when the whole island suffered food shortages, witnesses testified to the caring hand of God that kept the mission plantation sufficiently productive. Hungry neighbors, as well as strangers, visited the mission at all hours for food which was freely given.

Tini frequently traveled to the headquarters in Apia, where he attended meetings and presented reports from the work in American Samoa. One series of meetings, led by Pastor J.B. Conley from New Zealand, was held at the Tivoli Auditorium, a major theater in the center of town. Since these meetings were a major area-wide evangelistic campaign involving all ordained ministers, Tini remained in Apia for the six months it lasted. In the meantime, Mrs. Tini, with the help of elders and company leaders, like Hans Voigt and Tafeaga, continued to carry the responsibility for the work in Tutuila.

While attending a "Fono" session in Apia during their first year at Satala, Tini received a cablegram from his family in American Samoa. Florence, his oldest daughter, had contracted typhoid fever. She had been hospitalized, and remained seriously ill for several weeks. The American military-run hospital was completely filled and overflowing with patients in similar conditions, and was understaffed. To assure proper personal care of each patient, relatives were called and encouraged to remain with them.

Pastor and Mrs. Tini with their children and Ms. Kilroy, a visiting teacher from New Zealand, and trusty "sipi" in the foreground. 1954.

God's guidance was assured during this crisis. After being in the hospital for several weeks, Florence was discharged home, apparently healthy. Within a few days, Man-Ha Marjory, Tini's youngest daughter became ill. She was hospitalized and remained in very serious condition for several weeks with the same dreaded disease. Within a few weeks, Man-Ha fully recovered, and she was discharged to her parents' care.

At one point during these early years, Tini was hospitalized for eight months with a respiratory condition. At the hospital, Tini met and befriended some of the earliest Adventist converts on this island. During his confinement, he held Bible discussions and distributed literature among his fellow patients and hospital workers and staff. Among the group who were baptized from this work were Falefatu, Bob Hunkin, Sape, and Miss Rose Leutu Alai (McNeave), American Samoa's first registered nurse. Even with such setbacks, as illness, the family was well maintained and the work of God continued to grow.

One method of transportation across the deep land-locked Pago Pago harbor was the "paopao" (outrigger canoe). The Satala mission compound was located straight across the bay from the downtown district, making it a convenient way to travel fast and economically.

While Tini was in the hospital during this long confinement, his wife and children traveled regularly by canoe to visit him, to errands, or to do some shopping. A memorable experience h further testified of God's care occurred during one visit.

The two eldest children, Florence and Puna, always traveled with their mother in the canoe. But on this day, Mrs. Tini went alone. "Girls, I really need you to stay here. I'll have to count on you two, until I get back," Mrs. Tini emphasized the fact that the two younger children could not be left alone at home. She boarded her "paopao" (outrigger), and hurriedly paddled the small canoe to the distant shores.

After a short walk, Mrs. Tini arrived at the hospital where she met Tafeaga, an elder from Satala who had come to visit Tini. At four o'clock, visiting hours were concluded, and the two visitors left the hospital together.

At the wharf where the canoe was tied up, Tafeaga remarked uneasily, "I really don't want you to travel across the bay by yourself."

"I wish you could come along in the 'paopao' (canoe)," Mrs. Tini called out after Tafeaga helped her into the little vessel.

"Do be careful, and we'll see you on the other side," the elderly man called back as he hesitantly bade farewell to his friend.

Tafeaga watched the canoe as it slowly glided along the calm water, and soon Mrs. Tini began to disappear from his view. "You're strong, and you'll be safe until you get to the other side," the old man kept repeating his prayer to himself.

But by the time the canoe was half way across the bay, the unusually calm day had produced a full force storm. Waves and gusty winds lashed at the canoe. "The children are waiting for me to get home, dear Lord. I just have a little way to go," Mrs. Tini uttered softly. Her mind was focused on the Bible story of another storm, and it reassured her. With this prayer on her lips, Mrs. Tini was able to keep the canoe moving, rowing against the force of the wind towards a mid-bay marker buoy, which had been in sight when the wind started to blow.

The gust started to recede as suddenly as it had begun. A second buoy, this one closer to home shore, came into view, some thirty or forty yards away. It was now five o'clock. The trip across normally took less than thirty minutes. As she reached the buoy, Mrs. Tini secured the canoe to the side whi⁻

she bailed out the water that had accumulated during the storm. She remained anchored at the marker until the wind completely subsided, then continued safely home.

Tafeaga, who had hurriedly walked home during the storm, reached Satala. He had been afraid to scan the bay, afraid that he might have to face a tragedy that he could have prevented. He asked the church members who were at the mission if Mrs. Tini had arrived. No one knew about Mrs. Tini's experience until much later.

In the meantime, Florence and Puna had been waiting for their mother's return at the fishing wharf, a half a mile down the road. Neighboring women had gathered to fish at this location. It is customarily believed that fishing is most productive following a storm. The women were the first to see Mrs. Tini arrive, and what they heard and saw impressed them to testify of this wondrous miracle. They knew that no one could have survived this kind of storm in such a simple canoe. "God was surely present on this journey, and He protected Mrs. Tini through the whole ordeal," everyone excitedly commented to each other. What a marvelous testimony this was!

The first Lay Evangelists' class at Satala. 1955.

A Church At Last

As the membership of the newly formed "companies" grew, it became obvious that the little mission house was no longer sufficient in size for large gatherings. Tini's family had continued the weekly routine of removing personal effects to prepare for the church services. The need to expand was a priority, to erect a building to be used solely for conducting the overcrowded services. In addition, young people's activities grew with the increase in the number of this age group.

A local chapter of the Junior Missionary Volunteers club (JMV) was organized, and most of the adult church members became active participants, as well as advisors and instructors. Tini's young children became an effective part of the missionary team during the formation of the JMV. Most of the residents of Satala were young families with several children. Almost all of the young people of the village, in response to invitations from Tini's children, gathered weekly for JMV meetings and classes.

New members continued to be added to the church, and with it mounting demands for a single leader to shoulder the added responsibility. So Tini began to concentrate his time in training every member in the various responsibilities within the church organization. There were formal classes in lay evangelism, instructions in leadership and preaching, and training to work with young people in connection with JMV and Pathfinder clubs. Tini firmly believed that the success of the work of God lies in emphasizing the importance of each individual member's involvement and responsibility.

Up to this point, four well organized branch Sabbath Schools, in addition to Satala, were meeting regularly at the homes of certain members. Their enthusiasm in working for the Lord was evident in the way the numbers and ranks grew.

Again, the need for a larger mission building became desperately obvious.

At a meeting with members to discuss the options, Tini emphasized, "In order to operate effectively and efficiently, our mission objective will have to be shifted to a meeting place." Then he formally presented this proposal as it had been discussed and encouraged by the mission committee in Apia.

The decision was unanimous, that a "falesa" (church building) be constructed at Satala. It was also agreed that the existing house would continue to serve as residence for Tini and his family, as well as his assistant.

A unique opportunity became available to the church immediately. Tini had constantly been scouting the island for usable materials and equipment. Presently, the United States military was gradually removing supplies used during the war years. Many of the warehouses and storage places were being emptied out, or were unoccupied. One of these large maintenance buildings in the military airbase at Tafuna was being dismantled. Large quantity of the usable materials was available for sale. Armed with such limited church funds but with faith and determination, Tini presented to the owners a sealed bid offer of one hundred and sixty four dollars (US$164) for all the available material. As he was leaving the building, Tini prayed softly, "You know the answer already, God. I thank you for giving me faith to present my request with confidence."

The answer was immediate. The offer had quickly been accepted and without hesitation. Soon the church members began the work of dismantling the old building and transporting it to the Satala location. Tafeaga and Taufao, both church elders, were chosen as "tufuga" (construction chiefs), and so the second building phase of the work in American Samoa began.

Every church member took part in the work, and the new church building was completed within a few weeks. A new phase of the mission work on American Samoa was now beginning. On August 21, 1949, the Adventist Church became formally organized in Satala, with the four original charter members: Tini, Mrs. Tini, Mrs. Ufanua Bird, and Mr. Pasi Pasi.

In addition, each of the twenty-seven baptized members were voted in and accepted as the original registered members. By the year 1951, when the second phase and the new church building began construction, membership had doubled.

On this memorable day to dedicate the new church organization, Tini reflected on the uncertainties and challenges, as well as difficulties encountered in bringing the work of God on these islands this far. But ahead, he presented even more challenges and reassurances of greater success. He prayed out loud, "Lord, guide us into the next phase of Your work." And the people answered in unison, "Amen!"

As the celebration concluded, Tini renewed his vow as he prayed, "We have the rest of American Samoa to light. It's also the tougher part of this work, but You assured us You'll lead the way."

Manu'a, Amerika Samoa

The Manu'a Group comprises the eastern-most islands of American Samoa. It consists of Ofu, Olosega, and Ta'u. Until recently, none of the Manu'a islands had roads or motorized vehicles.

In the early years of Adventism in American Samoa, Tini's visits to Manu'a were few and far apart. These islands were isolated mainly by the lack of transportation between them and the main port of Tutuila. There were no developed harbors or piers, and the "shallows" between land and the reef were long and treacherous. Inter-island vessels which traveled to Manu'a would drop anchor by the breakers to avoid running aground.

If a trip was planned, then a message was sent ahead of the arrival from Tutuila. Thus the islanders would quickly and anxiously prepare for the occasion. As soon as the boat was visible on the horizon, able-bodied men and women went out in "alia" (dinghies or long boat) and "paopao" (outriggers) to meet and transport the passengers and their cargo to land.

The rowboat trip was often hazardous, depending on the tide and the condition of the sea. They often capsized on the way in, so the passengers and the cargo made a flotilla to shore. If the whole village population was involved, then they presented an overwhelming sight. Fatalities, however, was uncommon.

Under these conditions, Tini was introduced to Manu'a. On his first trip, he befriended a young man returning home from a visit to Tutuila. During the eight hour trip, Tini shared his food and drinks with this young man as they talked of many things.

"I'm a minister of the gospel, and this is my first trip to your islands." Tini was glad to point to the young man that he was unfamiliar with the area.

The young man expressed concern, and almost a pity for this stranger as he said, "You really don't know much about Manu'a." He thought for a moment, then continued, "My particular island is very small and rugged." He paused for a long minute, as he looked out over the star-filled horizon. When he next spoke, he seemed to warn, " At times, the people are also rugged and primitive." Tini remained attentive as he expressed his interest in everything that was said.

Mrs. Tini with some of the children getting ready to move to Western Samoa. 1956.

As they neared their destination, the young man commented, his expression more light-hearted, "I don't take this trip very often, mainly because it's inconvenient. My trips are far between."

The two talked all through the trip, and Tini was thankful he was able to learn a great deal about Manu'a and its people. When the vessel anchored, the passengers and cargo were loaded on to the smaller boats. Tini's young friend helped him with his heavy load of equipment, and remained with it until they were safely ashore.

"May these islands treat you well and fair, my friend. 'Ia manuia lau malaga' (May your journey be blessed)," the young man bade Tini farewell, then proceeded on to a nearby "fale" (hut). "By the way, by foot is the only means to travel on land," he called to Tini over his shoulders.

This was the island of Ta'u, the largest and farthest east. Pupuali'i, a lay worker from Tutuila, and his family, had recently arrived and was holding evangelistic meetings every evening. The attendance had been overwhelming. When Tini arrived with slides and films for illustration, more people pushed their way inside to see the "malamalama" (picture show). This was all new and interesting, and the people were becoming curious of the new message.

Manu'a islanders were strictly London Missionary Society Christians ("Lotu Ta'iti" — so called because it was believed that the first missionaries came from or by way of Tahiti, but traditionally, these are Congregationalists). When the new information and interpretation of the Bible was introduced, it stirred the minds of many. The meetings also became a delightful break from the daily routines. For the duration of the series, the plantation crews returned to their homes unusually early. They cleaned, dressed and ate, then they came amass to crowd the meeting house, to learn, and to see the "thin man with his 'malamalama' (picture show)."

Ta'u became the headquarters for this trip to Manu'a. After several weeks here, Tini heard of a long boat trip preparing for the neighboring islands. He obtained passage on the trip, arriving at Olosega, immediately to the west, on the same evening. Word quickly spread about the "'faife'au Aso Fitu' (Adventist minister) and his 'malamalama' (picture show)."

Tini was received at the home of High Chief Ape. Before dark, the family noticed that people were gathering in front of the house. The chief was amazed at the enthusiastic villagers, who came without being summoned. The guest, however, had traveled long hours and needed rest. The crowd was quickly dispersed after being told when to come back. The following day, everyone returned to pack the large open "fale" (house), and the meeting and Bible study lasted almost until morning.

During this time, Manu'a was suffering from food shortages. The villagers regulated movements in and out of the well guarded plantations. "Leoleo" (sentries) were placed at the common crossroads, where the paths intersected which led to individual plantations. Work crews started early before the sun arose. At five o'clock in the afternoon, everyone was to check back at this point on their way home.

One day, the sentries were startled when the workers returned at three o'clock. They asked, "Why so early? There's a lot of good working light left." The reply came in unison, "We want to get ready for the 'sauniga' (meeting)."

That evening nearly the whole village population showed up at the service. As usual, a film strip was shown at the end, then a lengthy question and answer session followed as requested. The people returned the next evening, but Tini needed to proceed to the island of Ofu, before the projector's battery went dead.

Tini left for Ofu that same day, not knowing who he would meet or where he might stay for the night. As he walked down the path towards the village, he prayed silently. He told himself that he would stop with the first person that calls "talofa lava" (Greetings!) to him (the Samoan custom of welcoming and showing hospitality to strangers). "Now that I'm here, impress upon these people the importance of Your message I carry," Tini recited under his breath.

At the end of the trail, Tini found the village teaming at work. It was the day to mend and prepare the long boats. At the center of the work crew, the leader and organizer was the minister of the village church. "Talofa lava! (Greetings!)You're very welcome to our village," Pastor Tauoa called out to the stranger, inviting him to his house. Then as customary, the leader insisted that Tini stay at his home for the duration of his visit.

Tini explained that he was a Seventh-day Adventist minister, on his first visit to these islands. The kind host seemed pleased, and he was quite excited. Tini felt welcomed and encouraged by it. Pastor Tauoa was thoughtful and almost nostalgic as he related his stories.

"I'm quite familiar with the 'Lotu Aso Fitu' (Adventist Church), because of the great work they're doing in New Guinea." He paused and pondered his past experience, then added, "I was a missionary there for my church for several years." The two leaders enjoyed their informal discussion that followed. Tini felt as if he had known this kind man for a long time.

In the evening, Tini held a well attended service and Bible study at this home. The only chairs in the house were used by the host, the village chief, and the guest. The slide projector occupied the only table. The rest of the space in the open "fale" (house) was filled with people of all ages, squeezed in so they could hear and see.

The following day was Sabbath (Saturday), so Tini rested at home while his host visited his parishioners. On Sunday, Tini attended the village church. After the noon meal, several young men were sent to help Tini across to another village for a brief visit, before returning to Olosega.

At Sili, a village on the north side of Olosega, Tini briefly called on the minister and his family. Finally, he returned to the village of Olosega, where he conducted one more meeting, then on to Ta'u before returning to Tutuila on the following week.

Rocks & Parables & Pulou Samana

On the next visit to Manu'a, Tini took Pulou Samana, another lay worker from Tutuila and went to Ta'u. Their first priority was to distribute the TALA MONI (The "True Word" magazine), and to contact every household of the upcoming evangelistic meetings.

From the start, the two men encountered opposition. At the village where the campaign was to be held, the Protestant minister banned the meetings from being conducted at any private home.

"But we're using the 'malae' (the large open green in the center of the village), not any specific home." The visitors emphasized that some villagers had pointed this out to them already.

While preparing for the service, the missionaries were again summoned. "The 'malae' isn't available for your meetings. Furthermore, these villagers are sincere Christians and they're part of my responsibility," a deacon sent by the pastor was quick to emphasize his importance in the community.

Bert Williams, the medical officer on Ta'u at the time, and a prominent village leader, kindly intervened. He invited the visitors to move the meeting to the hospital grounds. "This is public property, and your meetings are open to everyone," Mr. Williams reasoned, hoping to avert any unfortunate incidence. However, the devil was also diligent at his task to disrupt.

The minister's attitude shocked and disappointed the villagers. They became confused, and bitterly responded by throwing rocks at the medical facilities. The disturbance, however, did not deter the preaching of the word of God. "We'll continue

One of the first "graduations" from the "Voice of Prophecy" correspondence course. 1958.

to proclaim Your true message," Tini prayed out loud during the service. Turning to the congregation, he simply stated, "If anyone here is afraid to stand up to Satan, you're welcome to leave quietly. Otherwise, we'll sing together." With this brief comment, Tini continued the service, and it lasted late into the night.

Early the next morning, Tini and Pulou awoke, uncertainties almost overcoming them. Events of the previous evening kept surfacing in their minds, almost clouding any new prospects of the day ahead. They had planned to return to Pago Pago on the next transport, about two weeks away. This morning the two men sat looking at each other, each asking the same question of the other, "What are we going to do now?"

Still, the missionaries had no doubts God had definite plans for the rest of the visit. In their personal devotions, each prayed for an indication that these plans were still God's and they were keeping His schedule according to His time. While still on their knees, the answer appeared.

At the village of Papatea, a short walking distance from where the two men were staying, the only secondary school for Manu'a was located. The principal from this school had been at the meeting on the previous night. He felt embarrassed by the disorderly behavior of his villagers, and was sad to think such good opportunity to see and hear new things could be so rudely interrupted. This morning he was compelled to gather his students and asked if they would be willing to invite the strangers to continue the services in the school building. Furthermore, he asked for volunteers to guard the surrounding compound. To his pleasant surprise, the whole school willingly volunteered.

It was a simple request the principal presented to Tini and Pulou. "You're welcome to continue the services at our high school grounds," the man stated matter-of-factly, but with gentleness in his voice. His mannerism projected kindness and open-mindedness. "You won't have anymore problems from community leaders," he seemed to emphasize every word as he continued. "And by the way, the whole school will guard the compound," he added with a smile as he started to walk away.

As Tini and Pulou listened to the principal's request, joy and thanksgiving filled their hearts. There was no hesitation as the two men thanked the kind stranger, then they prepared to relocate to the school grounds. "God always provide paths where there are no roads to carry His message," Tini commented to Pulou as they reflected on the night's events.

By the evening, all preparations were done and the meeting was continued at the school grounds of the village of Papatea. There was hardly an indication of interruptions or memories of previous incidents. At these meetings several "a'oa'o" (theological students) visiting from the Protestant seminary at Malua (Western Samoa) attended. These men were well versed in the Scriptures, and seemed intent on disqualifying the Adventist teachings. They presented arguments against Biblical issues brought up during the informal session, sometimes directing their comments at Tini's companion. The educated men believed that Pulou was vulnerable because he was a new convert to Adventism. Unfortunately for the gentlemen, Pulou's knowledge of the Scriptures was no match for them. The evangelists were well prepared.

Finally at the end of one session, the group of "faife'au" (ministers) settled back, sighing with disappointment. One "a'oa'o" (student) remarked despairingly, "Pulou, you're like the fox that went after the bunch of grapes." The man paused abruptly. Then continuing, somewhat cautiously and a sneer in his tone, "Even with all his cunning maneuvering, the fox couldn't reach the fruits and finally gave up. He reasoned to himself, 'the grapes are probably sour anyway.'"

Pulou was aroused as from a stupor. He replied calmly and with confidence, "So it must be with my former church." Then he related how he became an Adventist Christian, after convincing himself that his life was hopeless.

He told how miserable he felt when no one showed concern for his life and lifestyle. "I woke up every day wishing that someone would offer a way to improve my outlook, my life. I did the worst imaginable things. I drank alcohol heavily, and I was a compulsive gambler."

Then one day, a flicker appeared when a deacon came to see Pulou. The village "faife'au" (minister) had sent this man to inform Pulou that his name was being submitted for church membership.

"But what happened to the Holy Spirit? I thought He's to prepare my life first, until I become a changed person." Pulou was disillusioned by the knowledge that he was not really prepared. "Or perhaps the change will come after my name is on the books, and then I'll begin to attend church?" The thought was almost amusing to Pulou. Even then, all he could feel was confusion and increased frustration. Pulou's spirit did not change.

"If I'm not feeling any change, this appointment must not be genuine. Is it part of a joke you're trying to play on me or is it a test on my life?" Pulou asked the minister as he discussed his situation. At the end, he respectfully declined the offer.

To the ministerial trainees, Pulou emphasized, "This was the sour grapes I intentionally didn't want to reach!" The parallel was excellent, and Pulou presented his greatest object lesson.

Pulou Samana and his family have worked in the church for many years. He has continued to be a great influence to those about him, in the communities where they have resided.

A Sabbath Affair

Following the successful encounter with the pastoral students on Ta'u, Tini and Pulou went on to Faleasao, where they had set up a base of operations for this visit. The word of God had surely been successfully sown on Manu'a, with literature, Bible studies, illustrative lectures, and public meetings.

Tini felt that it was time to organize and conduct a branch Sabbath School somewhere in these group of islands, presently with a population of over a thousand inhabitants. He believed that the seed of his beloved gospel had been firmly planted, but now a lot of nurturing was necessary. It was imperative that personal contacts be maintained, and that any open lines of communications were encouraged so that word on the "sauniga" (meetings) was spread.

Manu'a was the last of the Samoan islands where no other denomination was able to enter, other than the church that brought Christianity to its people. Tradition held the belief that the first church to enter its shores with the Christian message would be the last and only one allowed to work in it.

This tradition was the main obstacle in trying to spread the message here. Ministers and church leaders used this conclusion to threaten the people of Manu'a. Thus the standards of Christianity was stern and restrictive in Manu'a, in comparison to the rest of the Samoan Islands.

After a new round of "sauniga" (meetings) in Faleasao, Tini and Pulou planned for a special evening service, with a film and the popular question-and-answer session to close the series. At the closing service, Leaisefe'au Aso'au, the first Seventh-day Adventist from Manu'a was baptized.

Leai (his name in short) was convinced of the Sabbath truth, and made inquiries as to how a person might be able to keep the Sabbath holy on Manu'a. "I know tradition is hard to break, but

I must do this right thing if I'm to be true to my beliefs," Leai mentioned to Tini and Pulou during one meeting.

The reply was given with the decision to hold services the following week. Rumors began to spread by those who were attending the evening meetings, that church services would be conducted on Sabbath, the next Saturday. The natives had never seen such a service, and were eager to witness this meeting. A "fale" (hut) belonging to Leai's wife was prepared for the occasion.

On Sabbath morning, the three men set about to conduct their service. By nine-thirty, dozens of curious onlookers began to congregate around the sandy shores near the "fale" (house).

The "fale" (hut) was located at the center of the village, and everyone who walked by would stop to listen. For Sabbath School, Pulou led and presented the lesson study, while Tini and Leaisefeau listened. Afterwards, Tini preached a sermon, while the other two men comprised the congregation within the "fale" (house).

As the worship service continued, the curious "outside" congregation began whispering to one another, but remained for the length of the meeting. When all was over, everyone went back to their homes, but carrying the news of the unique "sabbath" services they had just witnessed.

On the following Sunday, after services were over at the village church, a delegation sent by the pastor approached Leaisefeau. They asked whether he would leave his church to become a member of the one that was seen by many worshiping on Saturday. "You've been a strong influence in the church within the community. Do you really believe you didn't live with God's truth all these years?" the question was asked by one of the church delegates.

In answer, Leai proclaimed that here he had found God's truth at last. "I've never been so sure in all my life. There seemed to be a peace within me, that I feel I'm being led by the Spirit." At this point, Leai's tone changed, and he continued with confidence in his voice, "And my family has become very important to me," he indicated his hope that his wife and

An early Lay Preachers' Class in Savai'i, Western Samoa. 1959.

children felt the same way as he did. Leai continued with sincerity as he invited his village visitors to any of the meetings.

Soon persecutions started at Leai's home. His belongings were thrown out of the chief's house. His family was harassed and treated as outcasts. The same delegation from the pastor asked Leai's wife about her relationship with the new church. "Will you be an outcast with your husband, or is your 'aiga's good name more valuable to you?" The wife's response was emphatic, "I don't share in my husband's beliefs." Leai remained firm and did not waiver in his newly found faith.

Several days later, Tini and Pulou returned to Tutuila. Leai, an elementary school teacher, decided to go along. Here, Leai and his family, who followed him shortly, lived for several years while he taught school, both in public and in the church systems. Mrs. Leai and the rest of the family who were old enough to understand were baptized and joined the church soon after the move.

Later, Leai and his family joined the church's work force as a school teacher in Savai'i and Upolu, Western Samoa. After many years in Western Samoa, Leai was called back to teach in the church school on Tutuila.

Tini took several more trips to Manu'a as the message became known to these islanders, and curiosity led to requests and more enquiries for further meetings. On one trip, Tini started at Olosega, then went to Ofu, its close neighbor.

When it was time to return to Olosega, the tide was high, therefore too deep to cross the narrow channel by foot. There were no boats available to make the crossing either. Tini decided to rest on the beach to await the low tide. He soon fell asleep under a tree. When he woke up, he noticed that two men were approaching him.

The men had been curious about the well-dressed sleeper whom they soon recognized as they came nearer. "We saw someone sleeping from afar, but didn't realize it was you, Pastor Tini," the young men greeted the visitor. They explained further, "We're Adventists from Olosega. We became church members when you came here the very first time."

Tini listened as the younger men spoke of their conversions, the people that influenced their lives, and especially the reason why they were so excited about God's message. Their reasoning was simple, but their hope in the new way of life was sincere. Tini was touched by their simplicity and enthusiasm.

The three continued to talk on for hours, sitting under a tree on the beach. Soon, the tide had receded sufficiently so the three proceeded to wade across the channel to Olosega. From there, Tini boarded the vessel that took him back to Tutuila.

Back To Upolu

"Western Samoa is going to be a tougher challenge for us," Tini explained to his family as they gathered for the evening meal one day. He had attended the week long executive meetings in Apia, and decisions for changes had been made and presented for the workers. Upon his return to Tutuila, Tini called on the branch leaders from the different villages, then he presented the invitation to his family from the meeting

"After working in American Samoa for over thirteen years, and the rest of our family were born here, readjusting will be the biggest challenge," Tini mused as he remembered trying to adapt to the American monetary system. Most of the children have now been educated in the American school system. "Yes," he re-emphasized, "there'll need to be major readjustments."

For Tini and Fuea, this chapter of their lives was closing in success and triumph. In 1956, the American Samoa district had established Adventist congregations in nine different villages: Alao, Alofau, Masefau and Satala on the eastern half, and Nu'uuli, Vaitogi, Ili'ili, Malaeloa and Leone in the west. Adult membership for these churches grew, but the young people rolls increased so it almost outnumbered the adults. By the year 1956, membership had doubled again, from the opening of the first "fale sa" (church building) in Satala.

To the missionary couple, every challenge had been a blessing, and there were more to look forward to. Quietly, the two began to reminisce over events of the past years, and Tini remarked pleasantly, "I never doubted that God's work would succeed in a large way over here."

"Remember the difficult trails and roadblocks that we had to constantly leap over? They weren't so solid after all," Fuea added softly.

Tini and Fuea did remember a few obstacles, but they seemed minor now. For in their hearts they believed as God's servant did when he wrote a long time ago: "Those who sow in tears will reap with songs of joy. ('O e lulu ma loimata, latou te seleseleina ma le 'alaga fiafia')." (Psalms 126:5). There was a new chapter to be written regarding the race to complete God's work, and now was the time to begin.

In 1957, Tini and his family were transferred to Apia, where he was appointed to work at Vailoa, the senior seminary of the Samoa Mission. The oldest girls, Florence and Puna, remained with their own families on Tutuila. The other eight children ranged in ages from infant to high-schooler.

Vailoa was still a co-educational training school for church workers. Mostly self-supported, it was located in one of the most picturesque part of Upolu. For Tini, this was like homecoming. Here was where he had first entered denominational work as an instructor, then married, and later received the call to pioneer the work on the islands of American Samoa. His job now involved teaching at the school, and evangelizing this eastern end of Upolu.

The church owned several acres of prime land a few miles away in the village of Falevao, on the Mafa Pass. Here was maintained a "ma'umaga" (plantation) which supplied the school at Vailoa with the staple fruits and vegetables throughout the year. Tini regularly took a truckload of students to work the plantation, and to take a supply of food for the school. One weekend, the work trip almost ended in tragedy.

The Vailoa plantation was located on the far end of the steep descend through the Mafa Pass. One side of the road was protected by a wall of rock, while the other side was a sheer drop of several hundred feet, to a fertile meadow below.

The roads on Upolu were mostly unpaved and very narrow during these years. As the truckload of students reached the summit, a bus loaded with passengers on the way to town also reached the top, passing each other where the road was as narrow as a mere foot trail.

In trying to avoid a straight head-on collision, Tini swerved the truck to the right, away from the protection of the mountain wall. To everyone's horror, the truck stopped short of the edge of the road, with half of its body hanging in mid-air over the gorge. "Please sit very still to keep our balance," Tini instructed the passengers who were all sitting spread out in the back of the truck. "We'll leave the truck one at a time, ever so slowly and carefully," he continued in a prayerful tone.

With each slight movement, the soft ground that held the back half of the vehicle slowly began to give away under the weight. But with prayers in their hearts, all the passengers were able to leave the truck, unharmed but shaken. The truck was securely anchored to keep it from plunging. Immediately, Tini and another teacher who had come on this trip were able to acquire passages on the bus into town. There they proceeded to borrow a larger truck from John Ryan, an elder from Apia. The two men promptly returned to the site and safely moved their ill-fated vehicle back on the road.

"We came out here for a purpose, and God has been with us. We're going to complete this mission," Tini spoke with confidence that everyone was encouraged by the outcome of this event which could have ended in tragedy.

After assessing the damage to the truck, Tini saw that it was minimal. He quickly made necessary repairs, and the journey was resumed. When the work was done as planned, everyone returned home, thankful and convinced that God and His angels stood by when tragedy seemed imminent.

During the three years that the family lived in Vailoa, four of the older children attended the Adventist School at the mission in Lalovaea (Apia). On the school days, they stayed with their paternal grandmother, who lived on the outskirts of the mission compound. The children went home to Vailoa for the weekends.

Lalovaea, which literally means "under Vaea", is a suburb of Apia, and the home of the Samoa Mission of Seventh-day Adventists. It is comfortably nestled in the foot of Mt. Vaea, on which at it's summit is buried Robert Louis Stevenson, the beloved "Tusitala". Vaea overlooks Apia Harbor and many miles of the vast South Pacific Ocean.

The opening of the new baptistry in Apia, 1960.
Tini baptizing daughter Man-Ha.

Tini often traveled to visit the family in town, and always took along a good supply of fresh produce from the Vailoa plantation. One day while on his way to town, Tini lost control of his vehicle when the brakes disconnected and as it rounded a sharp curve on the rugged road. The tide was out, and he could see the rocks and boulders which covered this segment of the shore, with only occasional patches of sandy beach.

Witnesses who stopped to help later testified, some skeptically saying, "Invisible hands must've carried that little 'sipi' (jeep) and set it on the sand between the rocks."

Upon close evaluation, not a scratch or dent was found on the vehicle's body. Tini, his younger sister and her two year old daughter who had accompanied him on this trip, escaped with no physical injuries. Mr. John Ryan and his truck were again summoned to help move the jeep back on the road. After Tini repaired the brakes which caused the accident, the travelers continued on to Apia.

To String An Engine

Tini often refer to time as his valued friend. Throughout his career in the ministry, he tried to use it well, and it became his trademark. And the people he came in contact with lovingly remembers his promptness, one of his outstanding characters. Church members that were under his pastoral care knew to be at the "falelotu" (meeting place) by the designated time or be late.

One day, Tini and Fuea were on their way to the village of Aleipata, some forty-two miles east of Apia. The meeting was set for ten o'clock this particular morning. But the rugged road was in disrepair and was almost impassable from the numerous potholes. At Lepa, a village several miles from their destination, the travelers discovered that they were either to continue on foot or spend time to repair the vehicle.

After maneuvering through a large pothole to avoid a boulder on the road, Tini sensed that something major had happened to the vehicle's engine. He hesitated to inspect under the hood, but the smile on his face told Fuea that it was repairable. "The motor is about to fall on the ground," he calmly announced to his wife. He further explained, "The springs that hold the motor in place simply dislodged and broke away from the block. It won't be hard to repair this if we can find something to replace it." His last remark was more to himself. Tini stood up from the vehicle, the look of confidence returning as he gazed past his wife, who was standing near by.

Tini always believed that God never allowed minor mishaps to discourage His work or workers. And miracles kept happening as constant reminders of His presence. Tini reminded himself that he was still on God's time, so this unfortunate delay would not interfere with his present mission. A silent prayer went up from his lips.

The two travelers simultaneously noticed that a house stood close to the road where the accident happened. They watched in silence as a man from this house came out to investigate the noise, then offered his help. "From the noise, I thought someone had crashed into a boulder. I was almost afraid to come out and look," the kind man confessed.

After Tini introduced himself, he pointed to the vehicle, then showed the dislodged motor to the stranger. "Could we borrow a knife to cut a wooden support for the broken springs?" Tini asked the man, who stood with eyes wide open in disbelief.

The stranger could only shake his head, then he disappeared for a few minutes, without saying a word. Soon he returned with a two-by-four-inch piece of wood, long enough to level the motor where the spring was broken. The man watched with amazement as Tini quickly repaired the lopsided section with wires, then he carefully set the motor back in place on the damaged side.

The travelers thanked the kind stranger, then quickly reloaded their vehicle and continued on their journey, reaching the village of Aleipata at eleven o'clock. The waiting members anxiously received them, bombarding them with many questions about the delay. "You look like a mechanic from the government garage," one member observed light-heartedly. He noticed that Tini's shirt was streaked with dark oil and his hands and fingers stained with grease. "Did you have an accident on the way here?" It seemed strange that the vehicle appeared unaffected.

"Oh, we had a slight drawback that detained us while on our way." Tini briefly told the concerned friends of the accident, while everyone sat motionless. Occasional "oohs!" and "eehs!" indicated the tension they each felt.

"There was no doubt in our minds that if you were in trouble, God would find a way to bring you to our "sauniga" (meeting)." The members emphasized the importance of complete faith and confidence in what God allowed.

Following the services, Tini asked for some wood to replace the piece that held together the front of the vehicle. "If this piece is removed, the motor would just fall to the ground." Tini pointed to the precarious part, as the audience stood shaking their heads in silence. Those members present were amazed at what they saw; the engine was leveled with a stick and held together by wires and a string.

After making a few adjustments, Tini and Fuea returned home to Apia that same afternoon, and without any further incidents. There was not even a slight indication that anything major had happened on this trip.

Rosaries & The Virgin Mary

W hen missionaries from different denominations first reached Samoa, they were fascinated by the eagerness of the natives to help spread the new teachings. Thus, each religion began their work, setting up and converting whole villages and districts to become their followers.

On Upolu, "dark villages" of all or predominantly Roman Catholics were difficult to evangelize with the three angels' message as presented by the Seventh-day Adventist church. One such village was situated close to Apia.

Tini contacted a family who indicated interest after hearing Pastor Papu Siofele preached this message in an earlier evangelistic campaign. Tini was received with enthusiasm, and was able to hold a series of meetings in this home at Luatuanu'u, a village seven miles from Apia. At the close of the series, one of the guests took a daring stand and proclaimed her acceptance of the gospel. This was truly a miracle, since the guest was the mother of the hostess. This dear mother had come to this village to visit her daughter and family, and surprisingly this was the first time she had heard of Adventists or of this message. It touched her heart in a refreshing way, and she declared her conviction with much sincerity. She confessed that soon she was to return to her home situated in one of the foremost "dark villages." She acknowledged the reality of challenges she would soon have to face.

When the mother returned to her home, she was stunned by what she saw. For the first time in her life, she was afraid to think of worship. Her home was in order, but yet she sensed the confusion of her life. She stood in the center of her "fale" and inspected the familiar scene she had created a long time before. In one corner stood an altar, with a statue of the "virgin Mary" mounted on the short wall above it. This corner was reserved and maintained for conducting worship services. During the morning and evening worship hours, the family members all gathered here to recite the rosary and pray.

Pastor Tini with graduating theology students at Vailoa Seminary, Western Samoa. 1962.

Early next morning, as the mother was preparing for worship, an enlightening thought occurred. Silently, she prayed for God's guidance in dealing with her family. "Forgive my ignorance in Your words, which were taught to me as a child," the mother prayed. "Now give me the wisdom and the courage to show this family to You," she continued, her voice pleading.

When the family gathered for the rosary, their mother kindly but firmly told them to face her and not the altar or statue, which she had covered with a sheet. Then instead of reciting the monotonous rosary, they sang a song and offered a simple prayer, as they had never done before.

As their worship ended, family members looked at one another in confusion. Their mother simply explained, "At this moment, I do feel uplifted. There's sadness because it took so long for us to learn the right way to Christ, but joyous that now we know."

A few weeks later, Tini and a lay worker named Taumaia went to visit this Christian mother and her family. The house was situated some distance from the road, with only a narrow foot path leading to it.

The villagers had seen the "sipi" (vehicle) going along the trail towards the house, and had remained there for about an hour. As the two men started their trip back along the trail, they discovered a huge boulder, which would have required about ten people to move, sat at the narrowest strip of the path. The boulder had not been there before, but now the only trail was completely blocked off.

Tini and his assistant quickly jumped out to survey the scene. When they reloaded, they uttered a short prayer, then proceeded to drive around the obstacle through some thick underbrush. They were able to pick up the trail and onto the main road without further delays. The two men were confident that God always provided the way to keep His message moving forward.

Beating A Hurricane

The year 1966 set a record for heavy rainfalls and a devastating "afa" (hurricane) on Samoa. One Friday, it rained heavily throughout the day and night that every brook and creek overflowed. Empty stream beds became full flowing rivers, and new waterways were carved.

The following day, Tini was to hold meetings and to preach at the church services in the village of Sale'a'aumua, Aleipata district, at the extreme east end of Upolu. This was one of the districts under Tini's pastoral care. More importantly, it was a success story as one of his earliest organized churches on this side of this large island field.

Mrs. Tini arose at five o'clock early on Sabbath morning, for she needed to prepare the day's meals for the children. They were all to remain at home on this wet day, following the services. She gathered necessary items for the trip to the village. Mrs. Tini knew that with the rains, trees would be uprooted and other debris would litter the road. "Please put a machete and an axe in the 'sipi' (jeep), just in case," she had instructed one of the children. They were all aware of the dangers when traveling in this kind of weather.

The trip started promptly at six o'clock. The roads along the rivers and the coastline were already heavily flooded. There was always danger of complete wash-out when roads were no longer visible as such. Close to home, at Lalovaea, the water was almost waist high and the jeep barely made it to the highway.

Finally at nine o'clock, after three hours and some forty-two rugged miles of travel, the couple arrived at the church compound in Sale'a'aumua. By this time, the wind had started to blow.

The meetings took place as scheduled, then the group gathered for lunch and Bible study. By now, the wind was blowing furiously, uprooting trees or breaking off branches while the bare tree trunks were left standing. Abruptly, a loud crash sent a brief vibrating sensation through the "falelotu" (meeting house). A church member rushed in and informed Tini that his vehicle had been buried under a fallen tree. The huge "ulu" (breadfruit tree) had stood to the side of the house, and Tini had left the vehicle parked under its shade.

The "ulu" or breadfruit tree is one of the largest trees on the islands. It has many long, sprawling branches and very wide leaves. Its starchy fruits provide one of the richest staple of the Polynesian diet.

Fortunately, the tree had been uprooted and had fallen away from the occupied "fale" and Tini's vehicle. Some of the long branches were spread out enough to cover the jeep completely. Church members quickly lifted and then jacked up the tree limbs, while Tini drove the jeep away from under its temporary trap.

At two o'clock, shortly after the meetings Tini and Fuea left the church compound to return home to Apia. Soon they passed by Aleipata, a neighboring village. By this time, the "afa" (storm) was blowing in full force. Where the trees had fallen on the road, villagers quickly cleared them off. Tini later learned, after some limited means of mass communication had been restored, that on this Saturday the storm was at its fiercest moment and most devastating. While he was traveling around the island on his Sabbath mission, wind velocity was up to more than one hundred miles an hour.

After about an hour of slow but uneventful driving, the travelers noticed that the road was all but deserted. As they neared the Mafa Pass, the two unexpectedly met a large bus, heavily loaded with people and cargo. The bus was missing its roof, and it appeared as if it had been sheared off. The inside was littered with broken branches and other debris, and the passengers were milling about, dazed and confused.

A few feet ahead, Tini and Fuea noticed a second bus and a truck. A huge tree appeared to have just fallen and was laying across the top of the two vehicles. When the tree fell, the top full of branches and leaves had broken off and thrown across the road to the opposite side, against the oncoming traffic. Tini and his wife arrived at the scene to find this enormous tree trunk laying across the highway, supported and elevated at either ends by the road embankments.

The trunk just hung there like a suspended bridge. It was high enough so that people and the smaller vehicles could pass under. The first bus, with the top sheared off, had been too high to pass safely through.

When Tini reached the stranded vehicles, the anxious passengers approached him and asked for his "sipi" (jeep) to use as a platform. One of the men had borrowed an axe from a nearby home, and was preparing to chop the trunk in half. The rest of the travelers were waiting to clear the path for the vehicles to pass through as soon as it was safe to do so.

Unfortunately, after only two chops the worker saw that removing the tree could cause a massive landslide and further complications. The road which was already impassable to larger vehicles could be completely obliterated. The frightened passengers thanked the missionaries for their willingness to help, then waved them to continue on their journey.

Tini and Fuea proceeded to travel towards town. In the meantime, an "afa" (hurricane) alert had been broadcasted on the radio station and warning horns sounded. The storm was to reach Samoa at five o'clock that evening. The "sipi" carried no radio. Presently, it was close to three o'clock. The above incident with the fallen tree on the road occurred several miles from Apia, another one to two hours away. Most of the thatched houses along the way were already flattened, and almost all the trees, save for young bananas, had been uprooted.

The vehicle managed to travel safely through many roadblocks made by the debris. After a slow progress through several more miles, and within three miles of Apia, Tini and Fuea stopped at a church member's home on an errand. They spoke a few minutes with the family, had a word of prayer, then the two travelers prepared to continue on. The kind and

Tini and his "missionary truck" getting ready for a trip in Western Samoa. 1966.

concerned Christians tried to delay the trip until the storm was over.

Presently it was four o'clock, and the wind was picking up speed by the minute. Its over one hundred mile fury and the torrential rains had already created mud slides everywhere. Fallen trees, mud and rock blocked the road in many areas. Villagers along the way guided the eager travelers on, allowing them to pass alongside their homes, where there was less interference.

Tini and Fuea were eager to return home, where the children were anxiously awaiting their arrival. There had been no storm warnings before their parents departed in the early morning. For the rest of the trip towards Apia and on to Lalovaea, Tini and Fuea were lone travelers on the empty highway.

As they neared home, Tini noticed a coconut tree had fallen across the road only a few yards from the house, completely blocking the path. The creek they had just crossed a short distance back had overflowed, pushing the debris out and scattering it all along the road and in yards towards his home.

Some members on their way home from church had taken refuge from the storm at Tini's house. They eagerly came out to help clear the way for the vehicle to go through. The family and friends immediately gathered in prayer of thanksgiving. All the guests remained with the family until the storm subsided the next day.

Mudslide Evangelism

During the rainy season of the year 1966, Tini remained extremely busy with evangelistic campaigns in the far district of Falealili at the extreme end of Upolu, some sixty miles from Apia. The team consisting of Tini, Fuea, and two young ladies, Isa and Ulata, always traveled by Tini's "sipi" (jeep). They would leave the mission compound early in the afternoon of the designated days for the meetings.

One bleak and very blustery day, the team had to leave earlier than usual. "We must make it to the Mafa Pass before the roads are obliterated by mud slides," Tini had announced to his team when they assembled in the morning. "And I know that the chances are good every ditch and gully on this hazardous road will be overflowing. I would like for us to arrive at our destination before dark."

So far, the journey had been long and rugged, but had progressed without any delays. Soon they came to the village of Falevao, just past the Mafa Pass. As Tini had predicted, the gullies and ditches along the road were already overflowing. Because of the water and mud, the road became a slippery, very narrow path. When the jeep reached the narrow trail into the village, its wheels began to spin aimlessly on the slippery mud. Suddenly, the vehicle changed course and was headed towards a five-foot-deep gully. The engine immediately filled with water. And because the jeep came to rest halfway on its side, the right wheels became water-logged as well. The four passengers quickly scrambled out of the vehicle onto a higher, drier spot on the trail.

Mrs. Tini ran to the closest house for help. "Our 'sipi' is beginning to sink in the mud. Please, may we borrow a rope so we can pull it up before it gets any deeper?" She had barely finished speaking, and a rope was placed in her hands.

A bus loaded with passengers arrived on the scene by the time Mrs. Tini returned with the rope. The driver from the larger vehicle stopped and offered help. "I need to tie this rope so the 'sipi' can be pulled upright or it will turn on its side completely," Tini cautioned the other helpers. The job was effortlessly done and the jeep was back on solid ground.

Tini checked on his companions, and quickly examined the vehicle for any damages. There was none. The group said a prayer of thanksgiving, and after reloading everything, the travelers resumed their journey to the meeting place. The rest of the trip was uneventful. The host families at the destination were warm and inviting, as they opened their homes to the weary, soaking wet travelers.

A few months later, the Week of Prayer meetings were being conducted in all Adventist churches. As Tini was the vice-president responsible for congregations on Upolu, his priority task was to delegate speakers (ministers and lay preachers) to lead out in each church. Services were held every morning and evening, from Sunday to the following Sabbath. These occasions of spiritual emphasis were very special to the church members on the islands. The services were always well attended.

To help solve transportation difficulties, the leaders who owned vehicles were appointed to the distant villages, where public services were limited. The members were appreciative of the help. But even then, some members still had to walk for miles to reach the main road where they were picked up and transported the rest of the way.

On Wednesday, Tini was to conduct the prayer services at two villages of Falealili district, the turn-around point for vehicles. The villages of Salani and Sapunaoa were separated by another village and the Salani, one of the major rivers of Samoa. Tini was to be at Salani for the first evening meeting, and then proceed to Sapunaoa which was five miles away, for the early service the next morning.

After a light supper, Tini and Fuea, who had accompanied him in most of these engagements, left Salani at about ten o'clock. A prominent village chief and his family, members of the local church had invited the couple to spend the night at their home, then leave in the morning.

"I've heard that there's been a lot of problems with the roadway. We haven't gone that direction since it's been raining," the old chief voiced his concern for the couple. He paused thoughtfully, then continued, "I'm not sure what sort of condition it's in now. If there's any kind of problem, come back here, please." The two thanked the chief and went on ahead.

As they neared the river, the travelers noticed that the bridge across was closed and being repaired. Vehicles were rerouted over a field to a temporary crossing, which appeared to have recently been bulldozed to level it and to clear off debris. Because of the heavy seasonal rains, the new road was knee deep in mud.

When the jeep started to cross, the wheels immediately began to slide around haphazardly, then finally settled in the muddy road. "Oh, no! It's exactly what I was afraid would happen," Mrs. Tini exclaimed, fatigue showing in her voice.

Tini was unable to drive out of its hold, even after the two tried to push the vehicle. "I think we'll need more strong bodies and muscles to get out of this one," Tini sighed with resignation. He suddenly felt very tired.

The crossing at this point was a few miles from any houses or village, and the chance of anyone finding the missionaries in their predicament at this time of the night was very remote. Tini and Fuea decided to rest for a while, as they turned their hopes and thoughts to the only help they were certain would never fail.

The night was cloudy but calm. The only sounds that arose to disturb the silence was the slow murmuring of the swollen river as it flowed into the sea, a few yards away. It was now close to midnight. After about ten minutes, Tini and Fuea suddenly heard distant voices, as of people walking towards them from across the river. There was no doubt in their minds that the help they had prayed for was approaching.

When the group of young men and women reached the two, Tini and Fuea immediately recognized the children from the family they were traveling to meet in the next village (of Sapunaoa). The jeep was soon pushed back out onto the road and the missionaries continued to their destination, accompanied by the young people.

On the way, Mrs. Tini asked the young men where they had been heading at this time of the night. "I didn't think anyone would be out walking in this kind of weather. And it's very late at night?" There was a definite question in her voice. What they revealed was truly an answer to prayer.

"We were just sitting around at home waiting for your arrival." One of the lads began to explain, while others from the group nodded in unison. "Someone suddenly said, 'let's go to Salani (where Tini and Fuea had been for the evening service), then we'll ride back with the "faife'au" (minister) in the jeep'." When the young man paused, another continued their story.

"You know, we have a foot path that we always use when we travel between the villages. It goes along the beach, and it's quicker." He shook his head, then continued, "I don't know why we decided to take this road that goes through the bushes, and which we knew was being repaired. But he," pointing to another young relative, "said we should take this way."

The young man paused thoughtfully, and when he continued, his tone sounded prayerful. "I thank God for leading us this way, so we're able to find you." The whole group sounded a loud "amen."

When the group reached home, the parents were still waiting, and were relieved but surprised to see the two guests they had been expecting. Mauli'o (the patriarch) had told everyone earlier that Tini and Fuea were to spend the night at their home after the meeting at Salani. But as the night wore on and it was getting late, he had started to worry.

The elderly couple, Mauli'o and his wife, were told about the accident, but they were confident God knew how the devil was trying to stop His work. "God always wins, because He owns the work we're doing," the old man exclaimed. "All we need to do is trust in Him, then no harm will come to us while we're doing this work."

They were all thankful that their God had many more ways to deal with any setbacks. For Tini, faith and trust in God's ways remained his motto as he continued to help guide His people.

Dark Villages And Ghost Stories

Throughout the 1960's, the years of the most intensive evangelistic efforts, especially in the "dark districts," Tini conducted several "sauniga" (meetings) simultaneously in a number of villages. At times, these meetings lasted for a week in four or five different locations.

Memorable events occurred while working in the villages of Lefaga and Savaia in the west end of Upolu, and Vavau and Lotofaga on the eastern end. This meant that Tini alternately spent two days at each end of the island during the week days. The informal sessions that followed the services were always a delight, and often ran into the early morning hours.

During the course of these meetings, Upolu was saturated with tales of the "aitu" (phantom ladies) who supposedly roamed the countryside on occasions. However, those who understood the Scriptures believed that the devil was desperately trying to stop the spread of the gospel.

According to legend, the two "aitu" (ghosts), Letelesa and Sauma'iafe, were princesses who died many years ago. Their spirits returned occasionally, and a young woman who became sick or delirious from any disease was given "vai aitu" (spirit treatments). The natives believed that illness was caused when these spirits possessed a healthy young body.

Presently, it was rumored that the "aitu" (ghosts) had been seen around midnight traveling from the east in their poorly lit vehicle. But villagers from the western end were puzzled, because the ladies had been seen coming from the direction of Leulumoega, close to their ancestral home, between one and two o'clock in the morning.

"Then there must be two vehicles," people from the western districts insisted.

One day, Tini and Fuea went to meet with church families at Lauli'i, a village about ten miles east of Apia. The meeting ended, and the visitors left for home around midnight. They needed to stop at a "vai" (water faucet) to fill the "sipi's" (jeep) empty radiator,

Pastor Tini with two of his daughters at Walla Walla College graduation of the author. 1969.

which had started to blow out steam. The faucet was located at a remote corner of the village, where a single thatched hut stood nearby. The next morning, an eye-witness broadcast (by the family who lived in the hut), through Samoa's "ualesi moso'oi" (gossip), that the two revered ladies had stopped their vehicle at the "vai" (faucet).

The family insisted, "As we watched from the darkness, one of the 'aitu' (ghosts) took a bucket and went to the 'vai' (faucet). The other one remained by the 'sipi' (jeep). They were so quiet, they never made a sound."

Several days later, Tini and Fuea returned to Lauli'i, where the members excitedly related the events of the past night. "The 'aitus' (ghosts) stop at the cemetery by the road faucet, whenever they go through here," the villagers had told the Adventist members. They spoke with reverence, and fear was in their voice. However, Tini had mentioned to one of the members the problem with his radiator. At the mention of the faucet, the church brethren were certain the travelers referred to were the pastor and his wife.

"The 'sipi' (jeep) really needed the water." Mrs. Tini was familiar with this routine whenever they traveled any distance. Further explaining, "We remembered where this faucet stood, so we stopped. I went out to fill the bucket, while the "faife'au" (minister) stayed by the 'sipi' (jeep)." As the mystery unfolded and some of the members began to understand it proved more humorous than mysterious.

The following week, the meetings were held at the western village of Nofoali'i. Several young women had joined the team for this series. One night, the informal session ended well after two o'clock in the morning. The group started back for Apia shortly thereafter.

After traveling for several miles, Tini mentioned the need to refill the water for the radiator. One of the ladies who was familiar with the area, mentioned that there was a public drinking faucet near the school building at Utuali'i, the next village up ahead.

As they came near the village, the "sipi" (jeep) slowed down, then stopped at the site of the faucet. East of the school stood a large tin-roofed building, sleeping quarters for the "taulele'a", young men of the village. The men heard the approaching vehicle, then noticed that its lights were very dim.

"If you ladies can fill our water cans, I'll stay here and undo the hood," Tini directed his companions. "Let's try and do this as fast as we can, then we can get home before it gets any later." Immediately, the women passengers went out to fill the containers. Upon their return, Tini went to work on the radiator. The women began to sing and talked of the evening's events. The sleeping men heard this merry-making, and came running out to see what was taking place.

"Who are you people? One thing for certain, you're not "aitu" (ghosts)," the young men asked the travelers as they gathered around the jeep. The women were startled by the unusual comment, and became curious when the men asked what they were doing here at this time of the night. Then the young men related their story.

"We'd just arrived at our quarters when we heard the sound of the approaching vehicle," someone excitedly piped up. "And we noticed those dim lights," the excited voice continued.

There was a pause, while they all strained to look at each other in the moonlight. One young man moved in closer to the travelers, half hiding an embarrassed smile, as he said, "You know of the rumors about the 'ghost ladies'. Well, we're very familiar with those rumors and where they've been seen."

The men continued their story. When they saw the vehicle, they all became very frightened. Each person made a quick dive into the safety of his "'ie 'afu" (bedding). "You should've seen us. We crabbed whatever was available to cover our heads!" One young lad giggled with amusement, then repeated, "You should've seen some of us that landed on the wrong places or on someone else's 'fala'." (This is a mat made from pandanus leaves.)

One of the men, however, was more curious than afraid. He peeked out from under his "'ie 'afu" (covers), curious if the women were actually heading towards their quarters. "I was puzzled," the young man confessed. "The women went to the faucet, then returned to the 'sipi'." The lad saw the hood being raised by a man, then the buckets were emptied into the engine.

He heard the singing and talking, and decided to investigate. "I quickly discarded my covers and started walking towards the vehicle. That's when the whole group found some courage and followed me here to you," the young man began to chuckle, as he pointed to his companions. "You're certainly no 'aitu'!" The whole group now joined the lad, and they all burst out laughing.

After replenishing the water, Tini and his group bade the young men farewell. "Tofa soifua. Ia manuia le malaga!" ("Good-bye. May your trip be blessed!"), the young men chorused as they watched the evangelists reload their vehicle.

"Perhaps you can join us the next time we come this way," Tini called out after them. "And our meetings will welcome your presence. That way you'll know for sure that we're not ghosts," he added as the jeep rolled by their "fale" (house). The travelers continued on to Apia and to their respective homes.

On the following Sunday evening, Tini and Fuea were again delayed by a long session at the same village of Nofoali'i. On the way home as they neared the burial mounds at Vaitele district, they were stopped by six young men from a distant village. "Here we go again, probably enquiries about the 'aitu'," Tini commented to his wife, who was beginning to doze off.

When the jeep came to a stop, one of the men whom Tini recognized, asked where they had traveled from. "I thought I recognized your 'sipi'," the young man pointed to the vehicle.

"Did you just finish a 'sauniga' (evangelistic session), Pastor Tini?" another young man inquired further. His voice showed sympathy for the tired-looking couple, and he walked over to the passenger side where Mrs. Tini sat, half asleep. Later on Mrs. Tini confessed she barely could comprehend what was being said, in her semi-conscious state of mind!

Tini quickly told them about the meetings they had been conducting. Then he realized the distance the young men had traveled from. "And what are you lads doing out on the road, at such an hour?" Tini asked the group, concern showing in his voice.

"We've heard of these two lady 'ghosts' and their 'sipi'. We became quite curious, and decided to check it out for ourselves." The young men all nodded in agreement, then they declared, "We were determined to prove once and for all their existence." From what they had heard, they knew that the vehicle with the dim lights traveled from Leulumoega (west of Apia) around one or two o'clock in the morning.

Now they knew and proclaimed the truth. The men expressed how easily the devil was deceiving those people whose minds were pre-occupied with things other than the Lord's. But God did have a way to discredit Satan and his evil work.

Savai'i: Big Island, Big Job

Savai'i, largest and western-most of the Samoan islands, contains less than one-third of Western Samoa's population. Savai'i's more than seven hundred square miles is rugged, with the interior backbone of mainly volcanic mountains. Several volcanic eruptions, (last one in late 1900) left part of the island covered with lava, and a few plant life exists there. Where the soil is rich, vast taro, banana, and cocoa plantations, and fruit groves produce abundantly.

Savai'i was the land where John Williams, the "papalagi" ("white man") missionary from England first stepped ashore in early 1830's. A memorial erected to this Christian pioneer stands as an inspiration to the islanders.

Unlike the smaller, rugged, and mountainous islands of American Samoa, Savai'i's roads and trails traverse vast plantations and rain forests, as well as meander along the coastline of some areas. Edible fruits are abundant along the roadside.

During the early years of the 1960's, Pastor David E. Hay, missionary from New Zealand, was the director of the large Savai'i district. In the meantime, Tini had been transferred to the mission headquarters in Apia. He was appointed as director of field evangelism, and also of the newly introduced Bible correspondence department, which included the "Voice of Prophecy" and "Faith for Today" programs.

The many responsibilities made it necessary for Tini to travel extensively throughout the islands of Samoa. He visited many outlying villages, holding evangelistic meetings, and

Pastor and Mrs. Tini with Pastor David Hay in Southern California. 1980.

performing "graduation" services for those who completed the Bible study courses.

As usual, Tini tried to utilize every moment of these visits. He often held multiple meetings during each stay. People moved from village to village in order to catch one of the services. If a person missed a meeting, he would simply hurry on to the closest village to await the next program of the evening. Even spectators from villages along the road often gathered in groups and followed the team for services that were yet to come.

On some of the visits, as many as five meetings were held in as many villages, through both day and night, and as time would allow. Most of the trips lasted one or two days, but the team usually traveled the length of the island. They also maintained contact with all the organized churches of each island during the visit.

Because of the limited time, Tini and his associates often rested as necessary along the way, in roadside plantations or the fruit groves, and usually late at night. It meant that they seldom needed prepared meals, since the land and nature provided sufficient nourishments until they arrived at the next destination.

On one visit to the village of Asau, Savai'i, the group left late at night. They drove a short distance until fatigue overcame them completely. They came to a large coconut plantation, and no house was within sight. The day had been long and full of activities, and everyone was exhausted. Pastor Hay, director for the large Savai'i district of Seventh-day Adventists, at the wheel decided it was a good place to stop and catch a few hours of sleep before dawn.

Along on this trip with Pastors Tini and Hay were To'ese Ah Sam (at the time was pastoral assistant, but since early 1970's has been pastor and leader of Samoan Adventists in the United States), three ladies of the musical trio, and another young lad. The two younger men scrambled on to the roof of the car to stretch out their weary bodies. The ladies of the trio settled into the back seat to sleep. Pastors Hay and Tini each took a corner on the front seat of their vehicle. Unfortunately, the rest that the group so badly needed did not come very easy. As everyone settled down in their corner, an army (surely sent by an enemy) of mosquitoes began to attack viciously. The swarms were so large and hungry that it felt like sand being thrown onto one's body.

The team quickly gathered themselves back into the car and headed out of the "war zone." As tired as they were, the group miraculously found renewed strength to continue on to the next meeting place. Shortly afterwards, the group learned that Asau (the village where they stopped to rest) and its vicinities was the "mosquito center" of Samoa.

Tini took Siaosi, an adopted son with him on one trip to Savai'i in 1963. They arrived at Si'ufaga, Savai'i district headquarters. Pastor Tini was to hold special Sabbath services at Taga, many miles to the west.

Public transportation was slow and scarce, so the two men borrowed the vehicle belonging to the mission pastor. He, too, had been holding meetings in the area at the time. The men planned to be back at the mission compound by early evening. This vehicle was the only available mode of transportation for all those people that attended the meetings. Besides that, its battery was necessary as it was used to run the slide projector for the film strips.

At Taga, a village twenty miles west of Si'ufaga, everything went as planned. The services were well attended, and the reception was beyond comparison. Following the meetings, the members prepared for the noon meal and a short study. In the meantime, the weather had suddenly changed, from the calm clear morning to a raging rain storm. The villagers feared for the visitors' safety, because the rising rivers were starting to flood the roads. The meal was thus hurriedly forgotten as Tini and Siaosi, with two young passengers set out to return to the mission house at Si'ufaga.

As the travelers reached the village of Puleia, where one of Samoa's major rivers was located, the road was already impassable. Another church pastor traveling to the same destination in a large truck was stopped at the crossing. He refused to move his truck to cross the raging river.

When Tini and his companions arrived at the location, it was impossible to see out of the windows through the pounding rain. Tini heard the man from the truck calling out to stop him from crossing. "Please Pastor Tini, it's too dangerous," he could hear the low-pitched voice above the sound of the rushing water.

Without stopping or saying a word, Tini quickly turned the vehicle around and headed back towards the nearest village he had just passed. He determined he badly needed a way to cross the river. "Lord, help me think of something quick and simple," Tini prayed in silence. Out loud, he asked his "son" to help think of a way to get to the other side. "Anything, even if it sprouts wings!" he lightly chuckled. The others saw that he was trying to ease their tension.

The travelers soon came to a rock barrier between two properties. Tini stopped abruptly. He swiftly jumped out of the vehicle, stood facing the rocks for a moment, then called out to his assistant to join him. Pointing to the large rocks, he simply said, "Here is our way."

They began loading the largest rocks onto the back of the vehicle, until it seemed like the tires would flattened. Shifting the truck to low gear, Tini drove back to the river bank. The time was now close to two o'clock in the afternoon, and the mission destination was still hours away.

A large crowd of people and vehicles were waiting to cross to the other side. At the time, the road across went down through the river bed. A bridge had been built since then, which crosses high above flood levels.

Tini hesitated for a minute, then decided that God's business must not be easily deterred. He walked down to check the deepest spot of the road under water, then returned to the vehicle and started the motor. The crowds began to call out to discourage the travelers from crossing. They feared for the passengers as it appeared impossible that the small vehicle could withstand the strong current, and be swept away. During an earlier flooding, a large truck with its heavy load was swept several yards down river.

As the vehicle reached the deepest end, a wheel struck a crack in the cement road, and it spun profusely but was unable to move. The engine sputtered for a minute then roared again. Nevertheless, the wheels acted like anchors in the bottom of the rushing stream. Now the water began to fill the vehicle. The two young passengers in the back seats became frightened and had started to cry. Tini spun around and gathered them to him at the driver's seat.

"Your family will be waiting for you. They'll be worried if you arrive too late," Tini spoke soothingly. "Let's sing a song to help the car to move along." The children looked up at Tini, big questions in their faces. They seemed confused, but immediately they began to sing softly.

For Tini, prayer was always the lifeline that kept him constantly attached to His Master. With a prayer in his heart, he shifted the car to the lowest gear, then continued the climb to the opposite bank. When the vehicle reached dry level ground, the rocks from the back were disposed of quickly, and the trip continued without further incidents. When examining the vehicle later, Tini discovered that only half of the spark plugs were even functional, and these had kept the engine running sufficiently through their ordeal.

Everyone who witnessed this miracle testified that it took God and His angels, and a man with strong faith to make it through safely. The crowds cheered, while the travelers thanked God for leading them all the way. They arrived at six o'clock promptly, in time to transport the villagers who attended the seven o'clock meeting.

The travelers related their day's adventure to the waiting ministers. Pastor Afa'ese, the owner of the vehicle, was awe struck. "What manner of person are you, sir?" he half-choked out the words. Then he smiled and simply said, "Welcome back!" Shaking his head, he sighed, "My poor little abused car has sure been through a lot of miracles today."

Manono & The
Truck Challenge

In 1965, Pastor Tini conducted evangelistic campaigns in the tiny island of Manono, Western Samoa. Every Sunday for thirteen weeks, the team—which included Tini, his wife, and a mixed trio, would leave Apia at noon. On the beach across from Manono, the group left their vehicle, then travel the short distance to the island by small rowboat.

Upon arrival, they rested briefly and ate supper. At seven-thirty promptly, the song service began. By eight o'clock, the meeting house was filled to capacity then overflow with people of all ages. As usual, the Bible study was followed by an inspirational film presentation. And each service ended with the informal discussion that often lasted into the late night.

On Manono, a large number of the population was Roman Catholic Christians. Many of these members faithfully attended the "sauniga" (meetings) every night.

"It's so good to hear new things and discover new meanings to this old Scriptures," one visitor commented one evening. "I'm very interested in studying some of the issues that I haven't heard before. And the Bible is full of lessons we all need to understand."

Tini was attentive to the group of young people that had raised many questions in the informal discussions. He was encouraged by these challenges as he answered, "We'll certainly try our best to answer your questions as we study the Bible together."

One evening, the subject of the Sabbath, its origin and how it was changed was discussed. This topic was close to Tini's heart. He always believed this was the basis of a Christian's faith, just like when he discovered it and changed his own life. As he

Pastor Tini with American Samoa's Lieutenant Governor, Hon. Galea'i Poumele during centennial celebrations of the Adventist Church on Samoa. 1991.

presented the Sabbath commandment, it stirred and fascinated many people in the audience. But some people were disturbed by it and they became angry and confused. When the informal session was ready to start this night, some frustrated villagers left the meeting, only to return later and began to throw rocks and sticks at the meeting house.

The service was cut short for this evening, for fear that someone might get injured. The seed of the Sabbath truth, however, had been planted, and Tini aimed to nurture this seed when the time came. To encourage those interested in further study, Tini presented his "truck challenge."

"Any person who can find a text in the Bible, and prove that God changed His commandment to honor the first day of the week as the Sabbath, should bring this to the next meeting." He paused, then smiled as he continued, "This is my challenge to everyone, no matter the age. The individual who can do this will be given my brand new truck."

Ironically, Tini had recently bought the vehicle, which was desperately needed for his extensive travels. The old jeep had almost completely disintegrated. An observant young man had traveled on the same boat with the team earlier in the evening. He remembered seeing a new truck parked on the beach when he came.

"Are you referring to the yellow vehicle I saw parked ashore?" he asked, as Tini was explaining his challenge. Tini nodded his head confidently. The young man smiled back, a sort of doubtful smile.

The audience quickly expressed interest in the challenge, especially the young people present. "Ok, this promise is real," a young man stated matter-of-factly. He seemed sure the challenge was not genuine. "If someone can prove this Sabbath change, you won't try and back out or make excuses?" the young man pursued.

Tini simply repeated his challenge, encouraging everyone to seek help from other sources. "If you feel that there's been misinterpretation, we should all be able to hear that next time, too. Any doubts, any questions, we should all be able to try and examine them together."

On the following meeting, the congregation appeared silent and somber. Everyone indicated how hard they had studied and searched their Bibles for answers during the course of the week. Many even asked their ministers and priests for help in their search. They all expressed frustrations over such a simple task. Finally, no one was able to produce a relevant text.

"I've found only frustrations and disappointments where people questioned God, and the Sabbath was made controversial," one well-dressed man offered. This same man was well versed in the Bible, and asked many theological and some philosophical questions during other discussions. Tini maintained that the best answers to all these questions still came from the Scriptures.

The team remained on Manono for the rest of the night. At four o'clock the next morning, the group gathered their belongings and headed for the landing, where they boarded the first vessel back to the mainland of Upolu. The early boats were crowded with workers and school children heading for Apia. When they reached shore, the evangelistic group quickly loaded their vehicle and traveled back to town in record time.

Lighting Dark Villages

From the late 1960's until 1976, Pastor Tini and his team swept the "dark, back villages" of Upolu with the light of God's message. At the beginning of the campaigns, the response was staggering and discouraging. The citizens of these districts were known staunch Roman Catholic members or Christians from other Protestant religions. During these campaigns, the team of four or five people spent whole weeks at the villages where the meetings were being held. In the day, the group worked in the homes, distributing literature and inviting family members to the evening services. Tini often found himself detained in homes to give informal Bible studies as requested, or involved in discussions to answer diverse questions on both Biblical and non-Biblical matters.

Whenever this happened, Tini returned stimulating questions that motivated the curious person to attend the meetings and to participate in the discussions which followed. The short but intensive series were held simultaneously in six or seven villages, for this distant outreach, and because modes of transportation was very limited.

To counterbalance the stiff resistance from village leaders and their loyal followers, Tini and his band maintained their spirit of adventure, supporting each other with unfailing humor. As usual, their vehicle was a source of delight. Sometimes, feelings of frustration was quickly forgotten after tackling a blow out of one or all four of the vehicle's tires. Most often, these misadventures took place in the wee hours of the morning, and miles from any inhabited village.

One of these events occurred one evening on the way to a meeting. Without any fore-warning, parts of the jeep's engine came loose and began dropping pieces out on the road. Tini casually stopped the vehicle as he announced that the group needed to rest. Pointing to the pieces of metal on the road, he lightly said, "We need to put our auto back together before we can continue. I just thought you should know that!"

Instead of uncertainty which was beginning to show on some faces, everyone started to giggle as they understood, and they stepped out of the vehicle. Right there and then, in the middle of the road on a moonless night, the group unpacked the slide projector and battery and set it up on the road to provide sufficient light. Quickly and thoroughly, Tini repaired and returned the loose or broken parts into place. As soon as the jeep was drivable, Tini jumped in and prepared to continue on.

Tini consistently maintained his habit of punctuality, especially in stressful times when tension and emotional pressure was tight and team members tended to dwell on the problems they were facing. No one hesitated or strayed from the group, for fear of being left behind. This kept the group moving, and more important, it boosted their overall morale.

In other instances, each passenger developed the habit of watchfulness. If the group was pressed for time, one eye kept constant tab of the leader, especially during mealtime. The moment that Tini finished eating, the vehicle was loaded quickly, almost rolling to a start at the same time. Any tidying up was done along the way, or when they reached their next destination.

During these extensive campaigning, informal sessions always lasted until morning. Following the main service, those who wished retired to their homes. The rest were invited to remain for the informal study. It was always a popular part of the meeting. Anyone with questions, suggestions, or opinion was given a chance to present it. At times, some of the visitors who were overcome by fatigue would fall asleep where they sat. Some villagers who were accustomed to remaining for the late session carried pillows and "fala" (a mat) to the meetings.

For the team, extra kerosene for the lanterns was necessary part of the equipment they carried since most villages did not have electricity. The lanterns were refilled several times each night during the course of these lengthy sessions.

While distributing literature, Tini became easily involved in the villages' daily activities. A family was preparing a large "umu" (buried oven of hot rocks) one day. Tini happened to visit in time to peel the bananas and scrape taros, two native staple food items. Sometimes, the families invited Tini for the meal afterwards. If his time was limited and had to decline such courtesies, Tini never failed to invite the family to the evening services. All these invitations were gratefully accepted, and whole "aigas" (may contain half the village population) often packed the meeting places.

In Western Samoa, copra (dried coconut) was a major export. There were several occasions where Tini arrived at the village while copra was being prepared. This involved cutting the firm meat out of the hard shell (sliced and dug out with a sharp straight knife) and spreading it out to sun dry or in a "umu" (slow earthen oven). Tini often stayed and helped the villagers with this. As they worked and visited, the workers soon learned of Tini's mission and purpose of the visit, then they began to ask questions from the Bible.

By involving himself with the villagers, Tini was able to slowly bring the advent message to these restricted "dark villages." The light was penetrating the darkness of inborn religious beliefs and prejudices, and many people accepted God's word.

Evangelism: "Teacher, Teacher And Graduation"

The correspondence studies of the "Leo o le Valo'aga" (The "Voice of Prophecy") was introduced to the Samoan people in the early 1960's. Tini, as the leader of field evangelism, was responsible for directing this department for the Samoa Mission. He determined to utilize this method to stimulate and motivate the studying of the Scriptures.

For Tini, it was important to strengthen and maintain his ties and contacts with all the leaders in the field, whether they were ordained or "lay" ministers. He thus produced a monthly network of the evangelism pamphlet "Ia Outou O!" (translated "GO!"). It not only carried the translated text, but local mission activities, lay workers' projects, and world wide events, which all church members delighted to read about. The "Ia Outou O!" ran for the rest of the years while Tini was in active mission work, and only ceased to exist a few years after he retired from the ministry for good.

To benefit the population, Tini and a colleague translated into Samoan the twenty-four lessons of the "Light of the World" series. Another leader in the mission, Tavita Niu, translated the twenty-four lessons of the junior series.

After the lessons were published in the Samoan language, they were made readily available and were distributed to all the organized congregations. People of all ages and from diverse religious backgrounds began to study from these sources. Some Bible students quickly completed the available materials, and then requested further studies.

"We've hit a good string in the bundle which tie people's daily activities," Tini commented to his colleague one day. "A lot of people, both young and old, enjoy studying from their Bibles, even if they don't understand what they study. And the

Tini and Fuea Lam Yuen with their ten children, all graduates from American colleges.

Bible is a readily available book. Every family owns at least one."

Tini's friend observed in return, "And it's a most useful pastime."

Upon completing the last lesson, the student was sent a letter of invitation to the "fa'au'uga" (graduation ceremony). Co-incidently, the ceremonies were all held on Sabbath, as an extension of the church service. On the letter, Tini indicated that services always started at nine o'clock in the morning of this designated day. This encouraged the students to attend all of the day's meetings.

A leader from the division headquarters in Australia visited Samoa on one occasion. He attended a scheduled graduation service. To his surprise, the attendance was more than three times the capacity of the modest village church. The people filled the inside as well as the area surrounding the open "fale" (house).

"I didn't realize our companies were so large in these districts." The visiting dignitary observed the enthusiastic crowd and the reverence exhibited as each person pressed closer so they could all hear the speaker.

Tini pointed to the visitor that most of those present were members of other religious congregations. "They've come especially because they're being honored for completing the Bible courses."

"But how in the world do you do it, getting all these people to attend all the day's services?" The man asked, his curiosity mounting.

Tini simply explained, "I only do what I feel is necessary to further the spread of God's truth. He shows us many different ways to do this." The visitor examined the letter that Tini had sent to each individual involved.

The dignitary was deeply impressed, and he agreed that these services were effective programs that should be tried and utilized world wide. "I would think personal studies, along with public meetings could only stimulate interest and curiosity. And these graduation ceremonies to honor those that have studied hard are very impressive," the visitor further expressed his delight. He still could not fully comprehend the extent of this day's success.

In the villages where evangelistic meetings were being held, the lessons were introduced and distributed following the service to those who indicated interest. Many students were able to complete the twenty four lessons before the series of meetings ended. In some cases, special graduation ceremonies were held on the final night of meetings. Those who were to be honored would come very early, dressed in their Sunday best (Samoans customarily wore only white to church), anxiously awaiting the ceremony.

In the end many souls who accepted Christ through the Bible correspondence school looked forward with excitement to the climax of their search for truth, that of baptism. In the light of their newly-found faith, and as directed by Christ to be "light bearers", many have continued in the work to spread the gospel message, not only in immediate neighborhoods where they reside but also wherever they are directed to "go."

Preachers And Convicts

A nother major task for Tini was training of lay workers. If a group was to be singled out for their role in the growth of the church on Samoa, it was and still are the lay preachers. Guiding and educating them for the responsibilities they would carry was one of Tini's priority tasks throughout his ministerial career, and long after he retired from active ministry.

In his frequent travels between the islands, to New Zealand, and to America and wherever large populations of Samoans resided, Tini conducted classes for interested members as requested. These lasted anywhere from a concentrated day to a week. His emphasis was always on the working relationships between God and man, and man with his fellow human beings. Men and women of all ages crowded into the sessions, as they learned old and new ways to work in these relationships.

On Samoa, if a request was made to hold such sessions, Tini often assembled several church districts to one location. The enthusiastic workers studied, took examinations, and participated in graduation exercises. Many former students who attended new classes enjoyed learning new ideas. In any case, such services that encouraged leaders who were responsible for proper church functioning, greatly helped to strengthen the progress of the work in these areas.

Late in 1959, in the early days of Tini's leadership, a large district in the western side of Upolu opened its doors to Adventism. Tini conducted a "lay workers' seminar" at Leauva'a, a village fifteen miles from Apia. At the close, those who attended were challenged with Christ's command to His disciples: "Go and Teach."

Several weeks passed, then a former student decided to try out what he had learned in the class on witnessing. He had met a young man from a neighboring village, and invited him to the Sabbath meetings. To his delight, the young man enthusiastically accepted and attended church the following Sabbath. After the service, the visitor expressed his appreciation for the invitation, and mentioned that he had especially enjoyed the discussion of the Sabbath School lesson.

"I'm quite convinced God led me to this meeting, because I got answers to questions I've had in my mind for a long time," the young man expressed his pleasure. Then his expression changed, as he explained, "I wish my father could've been here to learn the same truth. Oh, I wish my whole family could've heard it with me." He sighed dejectedly, and at the same time a silent prayer went up from his heart. Out loud, he exclaimed, "This will always be my prayer."

God did hear the young man's wishful prayer. On the following Monday, the request for Bible study in this village was presented to the mission's office in Apia. Before the day was over, plans were arranged so a series of meetings, in addition to individual studies for the family members, were to be conducted at the young man's home. This was at the village of Afega.

At the beginning, only family members attended the service. As the meetings progressed, the attendance increased considerably, and the house was filled beyond its capacity. By the final service, people crowded the area that surrounded the open "fale" (house).

Among those who accepted the advent message was a prominent old village chief named Maulolo Kuka. He invited the group of new believers to meet in his home, and to organize a new church company. "Christ's message should be everyone's priority, and we must proclaim it from a prominent location," the chief pointed to the group. He scanned the happy faces around him, then he smiled as he continued, "I'd like to invite everyone here today and anyone else interested, to start meeting at my home. Perhaps in a short time, we might be able to organize our group into a new church company."

Chief Maulolo rightly sensed that the new believers, like himself, were excited and anxious to evangelize in their own family circles. His children and grandchildren, he silently vowed, he needed to lead them all to God's "aiga" (family).

For a few months, services were held at this home. Many of those who had visited during the evangelistic meetings started to attend the Sabbath services. The membership grew rapidly, until it was necessary to move to a larger meeting place. At this point, some of the members suggested that they build a "falesa" (church house).

The simple but efficient structure was completed in a short time. To keep up with the rapid growth in their membership, an un-ordained "lay minister" was permanently appointed to work in this district. However, Tini continued to oversee the progress of this vast work for many years to come.

The Afega company became an organized congregation after six years of consistent growth. Their experience was a strong testimony to the work of the lay evangelists, guided by the Holy Spirit.

Under very different circumstances, a well-known convict in Western Samoa learned and accepted the truth, and became a completely changed person. Matila (in prison for many years) became a consistent Sabbath keeper, to the amazement of those who knew him. In village discussions and gossip circles, Matila was often the main topic.

"Has it ever occurred to you that Matila is perhaps performing the best role of his life?" someone whispered sarcastically, to no one in particular.

Someone else had added, "Would it ever be possible to say that Matila is a true Christian, truly repented and converted? It'll be a special day, when this becomes reality."

Many people knew that Matila was a good actor and pretender, and his conversion was just one of his good play acting jobs. But there seemed to be an obvious change in Matila's lifestyle, and especially in his outlook and mannerisms.

"The air about Matila is no longer arrogance and spiteful," one person observed. "Instead, he's almost humble and even helpful. He seems to carry himself now with pride, almost as if he's proud to show that he's changed." The conversation here had changed course, like criticisms suddenly became enlightenment. Tini noticed that even those who were skeptics at first were now becoming curious.

From a nearby village, an observer named Sauila became interested in the former convict. Sauila was convinced that Matila, the ex-convict, was truly converted, and that God was helping him through this change. The Holy Spirit moved in Sauila, and he immediately began to seek after the message that had won Matila's heart. "If Matila can be changed, than I can certainly change, too," the man reasoned.

Once Sauila made up his mind and determined to follow the voice of reason that tapped at his heart, he easily convinced his wife and family to join him in studying the Sabbath message emphasized by the church which observed this day as holy.

"I'd like nothing more than to see my family and myself understand the true meaning of the gospel and God's commandments," the man told Tini when they met one day. "We're all convinced God sent you here to help us in our study."

After a week of study, this family together made the decision which changed not only their own lifestyle, but also that of the whole village. In order to properly honor the Sabbath, Sauila's family sent a request to the mission office in Apia, that a church be established at their home.

The following weekend, in May of 1962, Pastor Tini opened and dedicated the new work in the village of Sale'imoa, some twenty-five miles west of Apia. Sauila and his entire family were baptized, and they became impressive light-bearers to those around.

The work progressed steadily in this village of Sale'imoa, and its membership grew rapidly. Matila, the former convict, passed away after a few years. As a lay worker, his converted life became a strong witness for Christ's cause.

Welfare, Samoan Style

From 1964 to 1975, Pastor Tini directed the work of the Samoa Mission's relief and Dorcas/welfare organizations. This included the hospital and prison ministries. He traveled extensively in connection with this field work.

Samoa was devastated by the record-breaking hurricane of 1966, but the world wide response for aid was tremendous. The church immediately set to motion its disaster relief work. Needed materials began arriving from churches around the world. The large containers of clothing, food, and medicines, however, were detained at the government's customs warehouses.

"This can't be happening, when hundreds of people are in need," Tini expressed surprise and frustration when he received the unfortunate message about the detention.

Tini immediately drove to the government office, praying that he would be able to persuade the officials to remove the much needed goods to the church's storage. He approached the manager of customs, who asked where the load had come from and to whom it was sent for. "I doubt this load's for one person, but we have to satisfy all these formalities for incoming merchandise," the government agent stated, half apologizing.

"Seventh-day Adventist Church members around the world gather tons of basic survival items and send them where it's needed. This is an on-going process in this church." Tini simply explained the global mission of the church's relief system. "Locally, our ladies wear the green uniforms, signifying their line of work. They visit homes, hospitals, prison and villages, and distribute these items to the needy, regardless of religious background." As Tini mentioned the ladies in green uniforms, the official smiled, and indicated recognition.

The customs official was familiar with this work as Tini explained. He immediately signaled approval to allow the containers to pass without any import duty payment, and no further delays.

Upon hearing of the shipment of relief goods, one government official who was assigned to review requests from the villages, approached Tini and suggested assistance for the settlement known as Solomona Fou (New Solomon). The request had been given priority status by the government. It was deemed fortunate that the Adventist relief shipment arrived so soon; it was the first relief to reach the islands. The official could not find anyone else he could turn to for help in this emergency.

Immediately Tini began to organize relief loads for this request. These were the events that unfolded as Tini requested information on the group. The community consisted of natives from the Solomon Islands, in the far western Pacific Ocean. These people had been brought to work the vast plantations of the Crown Estates of Western Samoa, when the islands were under German government rulership in the early 1900's. A well organized caretaker of the land was a certain Protestant church.

Tini listened with interest to the request and was determine to investigate the situation. Arriving back at his office, he immediately sent word ahead to the "Toreka" (Dorcas Society), as the church's relief organization was called, in Faleasi'u-uta, the neighboring village with an Adventist church. Four ladies, representatives from the group, joined Tini to visit the compound on the same day.

Arriving at their destination, the group left their vehicle in the center of the circular compound. They proceeded to contact the community's chief. In an instant, the visitors found themselves and their vehicle surrounded by a multitude of children, most of them wearing very little or no clothing at all.

"I've never experienced such a sight of unkept and uncared for children in any village in all of Samoa," Tini explained after they had left the compound. His companions remained silent, each one seemed immersed in their own thoughts. Their hearts went out to everyone in that unfortunate community. One visitor later explained that the scene at the compound presented a vivid picture in her mind of the "primitive heathens of the Solomon Islands."

This encounter took place on Wednesday, and Tini knew they would require a few days to gather and organize the packages for the families of the village. There were forty households; their names were recorded and each individual was accounted for. At the mission, packages were prepared for each family, which contained ten to fifteen people. When everything was prepared and ready, Tini hastily returned to the community, with the four women and a full load of goods to be distributed. The preparations had only taken a day.

It was a big day for the villagers. Crowds of children and their parents flocked to the "malae" (village green) to receive the packages. Some of them opened the goods right there and then, putting on outfits they had just received. Words of gratitude and thanks were expressed by the elders in the group. To the amazement of the visitors, the majority of the villagers thought that the uniformed strangers were from the government.

As the missionaries prepared to leave, they were given fourteen additional family names, and a request for future visits. "Our family members aren't all present today," one of the community elders told Tini. Continuing without hesitation, he said, "But I'm sure they also appreciate your kindness to us as well. You're welcome in our midst."

When Tini returned to Apia, he presented a comprehensive report on this special mission to the government agent involved. The agent was impressed with the promptness and the attention these missionaries had given to his desperate request. He could only manage to repeat, "May God bless you," as Tini hurried out of his office.

During a follow-up visit, one of the elders related a bit of history about their sojourn in Samoa. Years ago, they were brought into Samoa by the German administration to work in the government's large coconut plantations. During World War I, a change of administration took place, when Western Samoa became a British Protectorate under the League of

Nations, and later as a New Zealand mandate under the United Nations Organization following the Second World War.

The laborers from the community were happy to be given several choices as to their future. Some of the men returned to their homeland, in the Solomon Islands, while the rest stayed on and continued to work for the new overseers.

Those who remained were given freedom to establish themselves wherever they could find land. They were offered the opportunity to become citizens of Samoa. With this new freedom, the group moved out and developed their community in the land owned by a certain Protestant church, who offered it in return for maintenance and other services as required. The young began to marry adherents of different religions in Samoa, and they lived and moved about freely on the islands.

The limited land allotted to the families for their use became unproductive after so many years. It became a problem for the villagers, because the plantation was the main means whereby they could obtain cash from the produce they harvested. It was the only way they had to supply the community with their every day basic needs.

Out of desperation, the group began sending out some of their able men and women to neighboring plantations, or to any place where they managed to find easy jobs for pay. What money they earned was pooled together, mainly to buy food for the whole community. The rest was used for church dues and other mandatory offerings imposed by the landowners.

In 1974, another memorable encounter with the same group of families was again witnessed by the "Toreka." Because of the limited amount of supplies available at the local societies of the organized congregations, the group from Apia was summoned to assist. Tini tried to attend to each request they received, and then would communicate with the village leaders about visiting the area to evaluate the needs.

A request for assistance came from a village eight miles west of Apia. "A thriving community of workers on a vast plantation is in desperate need of everything basic to survive," the note stated. Tini discovered that these families had left the larger plantation when their services were no longer needed. All natives of the Solomon Islands, they had no other homes but where they could find work.

When the present landowner decided to develop a plantation on his land, he offered a place for the desperate community to live, while they work the land as they had done before. The planter built huts for the families to live in. However, no other necessities were provided for. As usual, the able-bodied members went outside to find paying jobs, after putting a days work at the plantation. And the families remained poor and destitute. The hard-working community had no other source of help.

When Tini received confirmation of the request, he immediately organized his relief team. He coordinated his visit with relief leaders from a nearby village. For this visit, it became impossible to obtain personal information or even the number of families in the community. Any attempt to investigate the needy group yielded uncertainties. Despite all these uncertainties, the group of missionaries loaded their vehicle full and headed for the community.

Tini and his group left their vehicle in the main village, and proceeded on foot towards the compound. As they approached the circular compound, they noticed the crowds working in the groves. The group went by unnoticed, arriving at the nearest house, where they hoped to gain information on the residents.

Unknowingly, the group had entered the overseer's house and was met by the "faletua" (wife). She explained that her husband was out in the plantation, but was expected home soon. "Please, you must leave the compound immediately," she anxiously pleaded to the group. "You have to leave right now, before my husband returns," she repeated quickly, "and go out through this back trail." She pointed to a narrow foot path across the compound, that appeared to lead to the banana grove. She did not seem to want her husband to encounter the visitors.

The group appeared puzzled, so the lady explained, "I'm very afraid of my husband." She nervously hesitated, then carefully, as if weighing each word, added, "We're here to oversee the community and its needs. But if you're allowed to carry on with your work, he'll be angry." The pleading indicated to the visitors that outside intervention would not be tolerated or be dealt with lightly.

"The owners would surely dismiss us from here, and won't look kindly upon us for any other job, if they get word of this encounter." The "faletua" (wife) kept her distance from the group, and her eyes constantly surveyed the trail for any telltale signs of her husband.

Sensing the fear in the lady's outlook, the emphasis in every words said, the Dorcas group proceeded towards the back trail. As the group had to walk past a row of houses, they noticed the ramshackle conditions they were in. Their hearts fell, as they surveyed the people within the huts.

Tini and his companions walked on in silence, but he sensed the disturbed looks on all their faces. Suddenly, as if their next move had been pre-planned and synchronized, the visitors stopped in their tracks. Ignoring the warning, the group quickly separated into pairs, and they continued to walk towards the nearest homes. Each pair had managed to visit a couple of homes, when loud arguing was heard from one of the huts. The group retreated to the source of the commotion, a home where a young mother laid sick.

In the course of the unpleasant confrontation, the overseer indignantly lashed out at the group, now gathered around the house. "You've deliberately come here to steal innocent sheep from my flock. You're no doubt very good at that." His whole body shaking from anger, he added, "Our people don't need any help. I repeat, we don't need any help." His tone was unconvincing, and his angry stare was fixed on the two visitors standing directly in front of him.

To these accusations, the visitors simply but firmly replied, their attention focused on the sick mother, "We didn't come to steal anyone or anything. We became aware of the great need here, so we came to feed and give assistance to those who need our help."

In spite of their desire to remedy the sad situation they faced, the missionaries reluctantly left the community and returned to the church compound in the village. They shared stories from the dozen families and homes they had managed to visit that day.

The day's experience somehow further encouraged the group that returned to Apia. They did not hesitate to request further relief items for the same community. Through the tiny relief organization in the village, the church was able to contact a worker from the plantation who distributed the needed packages. This man bravely went to the village after dark, then as inconspicuously as possible, carried the labeled bundles back to his compound. Later, he would distribute these to the families whose names were written on the parcels. From time to time he sent requests for other needed commodities.

Many rich experiences of this branch of the work on Samoa helped fill the pages that repeatedly influenced and enriched different lives. The "Toreka" (Dorcas) Society in Samoa continue to be instrumental in spreading God's message of love. Its members visit not only those in the hospitals but also those ill at home. Their work also included prison evangelism. For many years, the Adventist members as a church was the only source of spiritual ministering to these unfortunate lives. And many lives have been changed because of it.

Wallis Island: Mission Extraordinaire

E arly in 1967, the Executive Committee of the Samoa Mission met to discuss distant Wallis Island (Uea), and the prospects of introducing the Adventist work there. Pastor Tini was appointed to undertake whatever job was to be considered for this project.

Wallis and Futuna Islands are in a group about four hundred miles west of Samoa, and under the protection of the French government. Their total land mass is approximately seventy-five square miles.

Pastors Tini and David E. Hay, then president of the Samoa Mission, immediately began planning for this mysterious new undertaking. A recent development in inter-island traveling had been finalized between the locally-owned Samoan Airlines and the government of Wallis Island. Some scheduled flights had been rerouted to Wallis for a short stop before continuing on to the Fiji Islands, to the southwest.

Tini promptly booked a reservation to travel on the first flight to Wallis. He carried with him a small suitcase and a portable radio. He hoped to check the area's reception of Samoa's radio stations. At the time, the work of the "Voice of Prophecy," the telecasts and correspondence studies under Tini's direction was progressing fast and strong on Samoa. Tini reasoned that if the radio's reception proved acceptable, the "Voice" broadcasts would be an added tool for introducing the advent message to Wallis.

Aside from the short discussion at the committee's meeting, the Wallis project was known to very few people. Pastor Tini unceremoniously left with Pastor Hay for the airport on the designated day. Mrs. Tini, the only other person aware of the trip, knew no details about it.

Tini and Fuea Lam Yuen shortly after they were married. 1937.

Wallis Island was one of the places procured and maintained by the allied armed forces during the Second World War. A large landing field and base of operations had been built by the United States marines then, and it remain in use to the present.

After a comfortable trip, the plane landed on Wallis. Tini disembarked and noticed he was the only passenger who did so there. He gathered his belongings and walked over to what appeared to be the receiving or customs building. The whole place looked deserted, except for a handful of men who appeared to be workers. They were laying around facing each other on the floor, in a corner of the large building, and drinking from what appeared to be a wine bottle, and talking. No one seemed to notice him, so Tini continued to walk towards what appeared to be a hotel, further down the street.

The people he passed along the way seemed to ignore him, and Tini was unable to understand what anyone was saying. Arriving at the hotel, Tini headed for the check-in enclosure to wait for someone who could assist him. A man who finally appeared began asking questions, but in the native language which Tini could not understand.

Sensing the difficulty, the clerk began to talk in French, to which Tini shook his head and said, "I can only speak in English or Samoan. I am from Samoa...."

At the mention of Samoa, the man interrupted and asked (in Wallis' dialect) the visitor if he was Samoan, and that there was a Samoan here on the island. This time, Tini understood what was being said. Motioning for Tini to follow, the clerk picked up the suitcase and walked out of the hotel on to the road.

After walking for about two miles, the men came to a village where Tini was directed to enter a house. Tini motioned that he would wait. While Tini waited outside, a very dignified-looking, middle-aged lady appeared, and Tini's companion approached her. Later on, she would explain how she had watched the two men walking towards her house, and became curious as to their intentions.

As the clerk began explaining in the local language, the lady immediately greeted Tini with "talofa lava" (greeting! but literally saying "I love"). Tini was startled by her response, then asked if she was a Samoan. Without introducing herself, the kind lady quickly answered, "Yes, I'm Samoan. But how long are you going to stay?"

When Tini casually mentioned two weeks, without further considerations the lady invited, rather emphatically, "You must come and stay in my home."

Tini was speechless and taken aback. To this point, he had not even told anyone his name nor his business here on this island. Neither had his host been introduced by name. But with his reception so far, Tini knew that God would continue to lead him where he was to go next for His work.

In the days ahead, Tini learned the story of Leogia (his hostess), how she came to live on Wallis. A native of Wallis who lived in Samoa had married Leogia's older sister. They decided to return to Wallis, and seventeen-year-old Leogia went along with them. Because there was no direct transportation between the two island countries, Leogia could not return home. She remained on Wallis, and in time she too married another native young man. Years later, her sister and brother-in-law passed away, leaving behind three young children whom she took in and cared for as her own. Leogia's own husband also died, shortly after her sister.

When Tini arrived, Leogia had been on Wallis for over fifty years. The children (two girls and a boy) were now adults with their own families. Leogia had never been able to return to her family and home in Samoa. As she talked on, Tini sensed the longing in her voice. She also expressed her apprehensions about the family she had left behind so long ago. "I'm sure no one is around that would remember me, or that I ever existed," Leogia stated simply but with a voice that betrayed her deep emotions.

Tini stayed in Leogia's home, easily learning the ways and customs of the people. So far, Tini had not revealed that he was a minister, or mentioned the purpose of his trip. He learned that the island group was entirely and devoutly Roman Catholic, even maintaining the secluded school for training teachers and priests. Young men from all the Pacific islands were sent here, including a few from Samoa.

The Samoans were always welcomed into Leogia's home, and she considered them all "my children." Those who completed their training returned to Samoa, never to be heard from again. A few were still in training at the time of Tini's visit.

Within three days of his arrival, Tini was proficient enough in the native language that he was able to speak and understand it in conversations. For the length of his stay, he visited different places of interest on the island during the daytime. At night, Tini spent hours working with his radio equipment.

Curious villagers often passed by the house to ask Leogia about her visitor. She would simply reply, "He's my 'tama' from Samoa. He's a teacher." ("Tama" refers to child — male or female, while coupled with "tane" — male, or "teine" — female, specifies gender.)

One of Tini's first lessons in local customs, somewhat embarrassing but humorously learned, was the native dress. The islanders, regardless of age or sex, dressed in a short sarong-like wrap-around. On the other hand, Samoa's "lavalava" (wrap) is worn mid calf (for men) to below the ankles (for women).

Some women and young girls, curious about the strangely attired man, asked Leogia why his legs needed to be covered.

They asked if her visitor had some bad leg disease or unsightly sores. The kind hostess told Tini about these inquiries, so he started wearing his "lavalava" (wrap) as the natives did.

One day, Leogia and Tini went site seeing towards the home of the island's king. They met the royal family by chance, and were invited into the house for a brief visit. The king was rather impressed with the stranger's mannerism, and he courteously presented Tini with a gift of native crafts, — a priceless fine mat, which was a significant gesture of hospitality and welcome.

Tini learned that earlier in the year, Western Samoa's Head of State, the Honorable Mata'afa Fiame, and the owner of the airlines, Eugene Paul, went to Wallis to work out the contract which established the route between the two island groups. To their frustrations, the visitors discovered that no one in the government of Wallis could understand their English or Samoan languages. And neither of the two visitors could understand the French or Wallis dialects spoken on the island. Leogia was quickly summoned, and she became the official interpreter during these lengthy business dealings between the two governments.

Unlike the Samoans, Wallis islanders did not use mosquito nettings to ward off insects during the night as they slept. But unlike the Samoan open "fale", these houses have walls. Tini was impressed when at night, the villagers took sleeping mats out to the beach front. He and his host family joined the sleepers, but then he soon discovered the existence of mosquitoes out there. Later, Tini learned that as he slept, the kind Leogia had stayed awake with a hand fan, so he was not disturbed throughout the night.

On his first Sunday on Wallis, Tini quietly watched the villagers as they made their way to the large, elaborate village church close by. He decided to join the group. After dressing, he asked for a Bible he could use. To his surprise, he was handed a catechism pamphlet, which he accepted and took to church with him.

Food staples on Wallis, like taro, yam, and bananas were cooked in an underground oven. A shallow hole was made, then hot rocks and coals were placed with the food in the bottom. The pile was then covered with leaves for an hour or so. After the food cooked, it was dug up placed on a shelf, where it was accessible to the family members. Mealtime was a matter of personal choice. No table was prepared for a group meal.

Another food staple was fish. Trapping and diving was a nightly routine on Wallis, where men, women, and children co-operatively gathered the needed supply for the entire village. The whole catch was cooked and eaten during the course of the evening. No food left overnight was saved, for all was discarded the next day.

With his first meal, Tini discovered that salt or any such spices was not used in preparing the food. His hostess was well adapted to her adopted customs. She prepared a soup, of chicken stock and abundant native vegetables. After a spoon-ful, Tini asked for some salt, which, unknown to him, had to be sent for from the village store. When it did arrive, he was surprised and amused to notice that all eyes were curiously fixed on the strange item. Later, as he began to understand the customs, Tini mused to himself that the only available salt was unrefined, and the kind of rock salt used only for curing meat and fish.

During the early days of his visit, Tini learned about Leogia's family in Samoa. Most of the names mentioned were familiar to him. They were mainly from the villages around Vailoa, the boarding school where Tini spent his first years in church work on Western Samoa.

"How would you like to go to Samoa?" Tini casually asked Leogia one day, knowing that she had not been back since coming to Wallis fifty years before.

Leogia was speechless at first, not realizing that Tini had asked in sincerity. As she regained her wits, it was all she could do to refrain from shouting. She calmly replied, "I've always wanted to return home, but never had the means to do so."

She explained how the islanders sent relatives to New Caledonia, a larger group of French islands farther west, to work and provide for those at home. Wallis did not maintain any industries or other money-producing endeavors. And the natives lacked the incentive to accumulate any material wealth or properties. Land and other possessions were an accumulation of the family or clan. Every one in the clan was provided for. The children marry and have their own families while very young. Formal education was encouraged till the age of fourteen, after which, for instance, a girl most likely was ready for marriage.

As Leogia expressed her desires, she told of how often she had asked the Samoan trainees at the boarding school to take her with them when they return home. At this point, she had given up hope of ever seeing her family and homeland again.

When Tini asked Leogia to return with him, it was hard to believe such good fortune. She had housed the trainees and took them in as her own, but no one had heard her plea. This was a miracle, an invitation from a kind stranger who appeared from nowhere! Leogia immediately began to prepare for her trip, and the whole village moved about excitedly, as for an approaching special occasion.

As for Tini, his co-workers and the church members were curious because of his sudden absence. Many sought out his wife, asking her where and why Tini had gone so secretly. All she could truthfully say was that he went on a trip. Mrs. Tini herself was not sure where exactly this Wallis place was. But after Tini returned, the whole story was then revealed.

For Leogia, her dream of returning home had finally come true. She spent one month with her family, till she and Tini returned to Wallis Island. While getting acquainted with her long-missed family, Leogia learned that Tini was a well known minister in Samoa. But she remembered what she had told the villagers on Wallis when they came around asking about the stranger. It was not untrue, that he was a "teacher."

After they arrived back on Wallis, the two travelers decided that with the families' permissions, Tini would take some of the children to Samoa. A boy and a girl, both preteens, were the children of one of Leogia's nieces. Two more boys, a son of the second niece and the nephew's son, were also of the same age. The four youngsters had been raised as Leogia's own grandchildren.

On the next scheduled flight, which came a week later, the group traveled to Samoa. Here Leogia decided to remain with her family at her village, even to the present. She decided to end her sojourn on Wallis.

The Wallis children lived with Tini's family in Apia, where they attended the church's school. Years later, two of the now grown teenagers were baptized into the church. One of the younger boys had been returned to Wallis shortly after they arrived. Another followed a short while later.

The mission to Wallis was surely extraordinary. Tini's experience there was unique, but with existing barriers of language and customs, and limited transportation accessibility, it remains unentered by the three angels' message of Revelation. Those islanders who managed to go abroad find new lives in larger, more prosperous places. Some do find God's truth there. Only a few of those that leave their island return to stay.

Wallis Island remains a sleepy, unmotivated, and a strictly Catholic land.

Postscript

In the year 1968, as Tini was involved in numerous evangelistic campaigns, he suddenly became ill. Doctors diagnosed his illness as early manifestations of the dreaded Parkinson's disease. Tini traveled to Australia where he tried to seek medical attention and advise, as well as spiritual encouragement from some of his fellow gospel workers. There, he was admitted for evaluation and treatment at the Sydney Adventist Hospital. To alleviate some of the symptoms, as resting tremors and stiffness, Tini underwent surgery for the procedure known as thalamotomy. Being a healthy person all his life, Tini recovered fast, and his normal routine was resumed shortly after he returned home.

For the next ten years, Tini maintained his extensive work load. During intermittent periods, he and Fuea traveled to America where they visited the children who had settled there or those attending various colleges. In 1976, after being in the work for more than forty years, Tini was due to retire from active ministry. But this did not happen as planned. For two more years, Tini and Fuea were called to direct the work in American Samoa, until a permanent leader was appointed.

At this point, the Parkinson condition and his age was beginning to take its toll. His steps were slower, and climbing stairs was becoming difficult. However, his mind raced on, and Tini's zeal for the work continued as he dealt with all situations presented to him.

Tini continued to hold lay workers' training seminars and classes in churches where he traveled between islands and countries. On numerous occasions, he was often consulted or summoned in situations where his expertise and sensitivity was needed. On a particularly unpleasant occasion, he had to travel to New Zealand on an official consulting capacity. He needed to work out some of the problems presented by the Samoan churches in that country.

A favorite activity which Tini had always enjoyed was helping in establishing new families. He performed many weddings in the span of his career in the ministry, but closest to him were those he had a part in blessing, those of his children and grandchildren.

When his replacement arrived in the spring of 1978, Tini took his formal bow and officially retired from active ministry. His work in saving souls for God will always be in his heart and mind.

Pastor and Mrs. Tini Lam Yuen make their home wherever they travel to. They still maintain homes in Western and American Samoa. Until 1992, most of the time they spent traveling between their children's homes, living along the Pacific west coast, in Los Angeles, San Francisco, Oregon and Washington, Hawaiian Islands, and those still on Samoa. Since 1992, Tini and Fuea mainly stay on American Samoa, as it has become more difficult for Tini to tolerate these long distance travels.

On April 1991, Samoa honored the work of the Adventist Church when they celebrated its centennial year since its introduction to these islands. Adventism entered Samoa when the mission vessel "Pitcairn" arrived in the year 1891. However, American Samoa remained dormant as the work did not enter its shores until over fifty years later, when the young Tini arrived.

In tribute for pioneering the work on the islands of American Samoa, Tini and Fuea were presented with a memorial plaque, a simple but heart-felt token of love and respect from those people whose lives they touched. The CenPac News (newsletter of the Central Pacific Union Mission of SDA) reported on the event: "A beautiful moment arrived, one that will always live in Adventist Church history. Although aged and ailing, and finding walking very difficult, American Samoa's first worker and pioneer on the frontiers of island evangelism, Pastor Tini Inu Lam Yuen came forward to receive the honor, thanks and love of his people for his humble and very effective service for God. He was presented with a beautifully crafted souvenir — a plaque exhibiting an open Bible with the text from Isaiah 52:7 (KJV): 'How beautiful upon the mountains are the feet of him that bringeth good tidings.' How fitting it was to see his wife Fuea at his side at this time. They were a really good team over many years of service in the Master's vineyard." (CenPac News; Suva, Fiji. June 6, 1991.)

Epilogue

Pago Pago, American Samoa:

Pastor Tini Inu Lam Yuen, who pioneered the Seventh-day Adventist Church in American Samoa, as well as many areas of Western Samoa passed away peacefully in his sleep at his home in Taputimu last week on Friday, May 10, 1996. He was 79 years old.

"My father was a practical and simple man," recalls son, Lam Yuen Jr. "He was considerate, compassionate and had the greatest respect for his fellow man."

Lam Yuen Jr. added that "education" was his father's number one priority. Accordingly, all his children are college graduates. "We are fortunate to have been recipients of educational scholarships," he said. "But our success is due largely to the encouragement by our parents."

The late Lam Yuen was born to Mata'iumu Tulifua of Taputimu and Lam Wu Yuen of Foochow, China. He spent most of his early years in Western Samoa where he attended Marist Brothers School at Mulivai. He became a member of the Seventh-day Adventist Church at the age of 17 and proceeded to be an ordained minister in 1947.

Pastor Tini is survived by his wife Fueainaula Mu Tagaloa Lam Yuen of Saoluafata, Western Samoa, whom he married in 1937 while still in the seminary. They were blessed with 10 children, seven daughters and three sons, 83 grandchildren and 36 great-grandchildren.

In 1944, while still in ministerial training, Lam Yuen and his young family came to American Samoa on behalf of the Seventh-day Adventist Church and eventually set up the first local SDA congregation, based in Satala. His ministry took him back and forth to Upolu, Savai'i and then back to American

Samoa, from where he finally retired in 1978. During his ministry, he served as evangelist, seminary instructor, principal administrator, and other areas where he willingly accepted when called upon to serve by the church.

His final services will be held at the Seventh-day Adventist Church at Iakina, Ili'ili, on Monday, May 20, 1996, with burial at his family home in Taputimu.

Written by Lave Tuiletufuga

SAMOA NEWS, Pago Pago, American Samoa

Friday, May 17, 1996

"Ua ou tau le taua lelei, ua i'u ia te a'u le tausinioga, ua ou taofi i le upu o le fa'atuatua. O lenei, ua teuina mo a'u le pale o le amiotonu; e le gata fo'i ia te a'u, a o i latou uma lava o e fiafia i lona fa'aali mai." II Timoteo 4:7, 8

> *"I have fought the good fight, I have finished the race, I have kept the faith. Now there is in store for me the crown of righteousness, which the Lord, the righteous Judge, will award to me on that day, and not only to me, but also to all who have longed for His appearing."* II Timothy 4:7, 8 NIV

Baptized Members To 1956

1. Mr. Papu Siofele
2. Mrs. Fa'auliuli Papu
3. Mr. Salatua
4. Mrs. Maletina Uta *
5. Mrs. Se'ese'ei Salatua
6. Mrs. Ta'aitumalo Taufao
7. Mr. Taufao Faifua
8. Mr. Tafeaga Auelua
9. Mrs. Siniva Tafeaga
10. Mrs. Sifea Ta'ata'ai
11. Mr. Ta'ata'ai Tupuola
12. Mr. Fuata'i
13. Mrs. Fa'ai'u Fuata'i
14. Mr. Palafu Falana'i
15. Mrs. Saofa'i Palafu
16. Mr. Fe'i Alo
17. Mr. Eli
18. Mrs. Fa'api'o Eli
19. Mr. Soga Eli
20. Fa'ataga Fuata'i
21. Mr. Pupuali'i Fuaali'i
22. Mrs. Emele Pupuali'i
23. Mr. Malae Talalelei
24. Mrs. Felamata'i Malae
25. Mr. Ve'ave'a Auelua
26. Mr Hans Voigt *
27. Mr.Foaga
28. Mr. Eliapo To'a
29. Mrs. Tala Eliapo

30. Mr. Fa'apepele
31. Mrs. Fa'aafe Fa'apepele
32. Mr. Fa'atiu llaoa
33. Mrs. Taufaga Fa'atiu
34. Mr. Lokeni Laupola
35. Mrs. Va'aiga Lokeni
36. Mr. Talauna Solaita
37. Mrs. Ema Talauna
38. Mr. Samatua Leao
39. Mrs. Malia Samatua
40. Mr. John Ufuti
41. Mrs. Aimeamiti Ufuti
42. Mr. Samoa Utuga
43. Mrs. Tala Samoa
44. Mr. Aumavae Toloumu
45. Mrs. Malama Mafutau
46. Mrs. Fetuia'i Si'uloma
47. Mr. Faga Pasa
48. Rose Leutu Alai
49. Mr. Falefatu Utu
50. Mr. Atimani Alo
51. Mr. Ieti Faletogo
52. Mrs. Laumua Ieti
53. Mr. Siaumau Leao
54. Mrs. Siniva Siaumau
55. Mr. Petaia Samuelu

> * Denotes baptized members
> transferred from Western Samoa.

56. Mrs. Tusi Petaia
57. Mr. Filiki Noma Foster
58. Mrs. Fa'ataitaia Filiki
59. Mr. Pulou Samana
60. Mrs. Fa'aitu Pulou
61. Mr. Robert Hunkin
62. Mrs. Nu'uuli Hunkin
63. Sinabada Talatonu
64. Mr. Filipo Lepulu
65. Vaolotu Samana
66. Florence Lam Yuen
67. Mr. Leaisefe'au Aso'au
68. Mrs. Pomaao Leaisefe'au
69. Fa'atupu Sasa
70. Mr. Sitaiai Ma'ileoi
71. Mrs. Meleane Filipo
72. Mr. Sape Sape
73. Legalo Eli
74. Mrs. Saumolia Puia'i

75. Mr. Silao Fautanu
76. Mr. Po'ua
77. Mr. Iakopo Fuata'i
78. Sa Iepala *
79. Mrs. Saunoaga Falana'i
80. Mr. Lee Asu'ega
81. Naimanu Salatua
82. Mrs. Ufanua Bird *
83. Mr. Pasi Pasi *
84. Mr. Uta Isaia *
85. Ta'e Samatua
86. Puna Lam Yuen
87. Mrs. Falefia Faga
88. Mrs. Seu Atimani
89. Mrs. Faiga Curry
90. Mr. James Weiden*
91. Mrs. Edna Weiden*
92. Pastor Tini Lam Yuen*
93. Mrs. Fuea Lam Yuen*

* Denotes baptized members
transferred from Western Samoa.

Glossary Of Samoan Terms

Afa	Hurricane or storm
Agaga	Spirit or soul
Aiga	The extended family
Aitu	Ghost
Alia	Long boat or double canoe
A'oa'o	A preacher or specifically theological student
Atua	God or a diety
Fa'a-Samoa	The "Samoan way"; lifestyle of the Samoans
Fa'au'uga	Graduation or ordination
"Fa'avae i le Atua Samoa"	"Samoa is found on God"
Faife'au Aso Fitu	Adventist minister
Faife'au Papalagi	A foreign minister
Fala	A mat made of pandanus leaves
Fale	Open house with thatched roof, customarily oval or round
Falelotu	Mission house; literally, "church house"
Falesa	A church building; literally, "forbidden (denoting sacred) house"
Fale Fono	A village or clan's main council house; the governments' Parliament (Western Samoa) or Senate (American Samoa) buildings
Fale tele	"The great family dwelling" or council house
Faletua	Literally, "house in the back", denotes the wife of a distinguished person, such as matai
Fono	A council meeting or an assembly
"Ia manuia lau malaga"	"May your journey be blessed"
"Ia Outou O"	"Go" magazine; literally, "you go"
'Ie 'afu	Bedding or cover sheet

116

Lali	A large solid wooden drum
Lalovaea	A suburb of Apia; location of the headquarters of the Samoa Mission of Seventh-day Adventists
Lau	Thatch or leaf
"Laumei ma le Malie"	Legend of the "Turtle and the Shark"
Launiu	Coconut leaf
"Lau Susuga Tini"	An honored title
Lavalava	Clothes; a wraparound, loin cloth or sarong
Leoleo	A guard or sentry
"Leo ole Valo'aga"	The "Voice of Prophecy"
Lotu Aso Fitu	The Seventh-day Adventist Church
Lotu Toga	Methodist Church or "Church of Tonga"
Lotu Ta'iti	Literally, "Church of Tahiti", London Missionary Society Church or a Congregational Church
Malae	"Open green" or grassy area in the center of a village
"Malamalama"	A picture or slide show for illustration or a projector
Matai	The chief of a family or a village
Ma'umaga	Plantation
Paopao	Outrigger canoe
Papalagi	Literally, "Heaven-bursters;" denotes a white man
Sauniga	Evangelistic meeting or service
Sipi	"Jeep" or denoting a small car
Talofa	A form of greeting or salutation; literally, "I love"
"Tala Moni"	"The Truth" magazine; literally, "true word"
Tama	A child or a woman's offspring
Tama tane/tama tama	A male child or a son
Tama teine/tama fafine	A female child or daughter
Teine	A girl
Taulele'a	Young men of a family or village

Tofa	A farewell; a chief
"Tofa soifua"	Literally, "Farewell; may you live"
Toreka	Biblical Dorcas; denoting the relief work of the Seventh-day Adventist Church
Tufuga	The construction chief or foreman
"Tusitala"	"Writer of tales", title that refers to Robert Louis Stevenson
"Ualesi moso'oi"	Gossip and rumors
"Ua sau le faife'au"	"The minister is here."
'Ulu	Breadfruit, a native starchy food staple
Umu	Cooking house; oven of hot rocks for cooking
Vai	Water or a faucet
Vai aitu	"Spirit remedies"

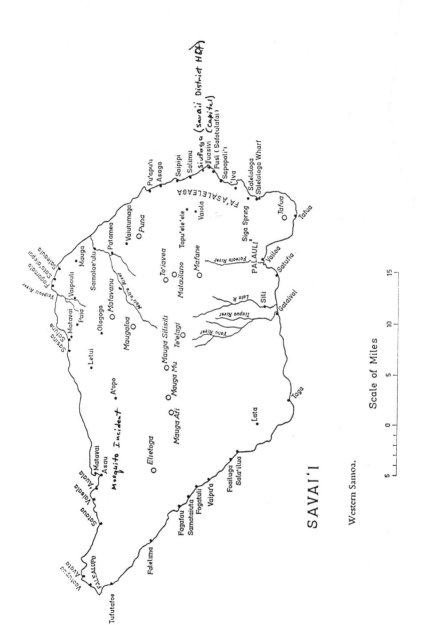

SAVAI'I

Western Samoa.

Scale of Miles

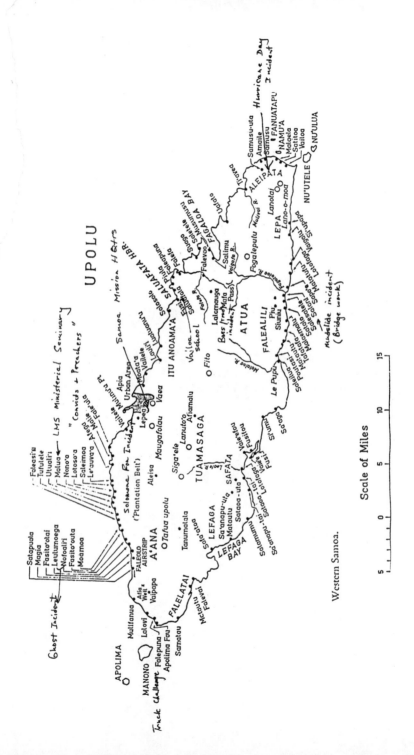

Western Samoa.

Scale of Miles

We'd love to send you a free catalog of titles we publish
or even hear your thoughts, reactions, criticism,
about things you did or didn't like about this
or any other book we publish.

Just write or call us at:

TEACH Services, Inc.
254 Donovan Road
Brushton, New York 12916-9738
1-800/367-1998

http://www.TEACHServicesInc.com